This book was awarded as part of the

2008
WE THE PEOPLE **on** Created Equal
BOOKSHELF

Presented by the National Endowment for the Humanities (NEH)
in cooperation with the American Library Association (ALA).

www.neh.gov   www.ala.org

Abraham Lincoln

The Writer

A Treasury of His Greatest Speeches and Letters

Compiled and Edited by
Harold Holzer

Abraham Lincoln
~ The Writer ~

A Treasury of His Greatest Speeches and Letters

JB
LINCOLN
2000

Compiled and Edited by Harold Holzer

CALKINS CREEK BOOKS

Boyds Mills Press

COVER: *President Lincoln, Writing the Proclamation of Freedom,/January 1st. 1863,* a print after a painting by David Gilmour Blythe. Lincoln actually wrote the Emancipation Proclamation earlier and signed the final copy on January 1, 1863. Courtesy of The Lincoln Museum, Fort Wayne, Indiana (#2051)

Published by Calkins Creek Books
Boyds Mills Press, Inc.
A Highlights Company
815 Church Street
Honesdale, Pennsylvania 18431
Printed in China

U.S. Cataloging-in-Publication Data
(Library of Congress Standards)

Abraham Lincoln the writer : a treasury of his greatest speeches and letters / compiled and edited by Harold Holzer. 1st ed.
[108]p. : ill. port. ; cm.
Includes index.
Summary: A collection of speeches and letters of Abraham Lincoln, with brief introductions that provide historical background. Illustrated throughout with black-and-white archival photographs.
ISBN 1-56397-772-9
1. Lincoln, Abraham, 1809-1865—Juvenile literature.
2. United States—Politics and government—1861-1865—Juvenile literature. [1. Lincoln, Abraham, 1809-1865. 2. Presidents —United States—Biography.] I. Holzer, Harold. II. Title.
973.7 / 092 —dc21 [B] 2000 AC CIP
99-66551

First edition, 2000
The text of this book is set in 12-point Goudy.

10 9 8 7 6 5

For Deanne and Susanne,
who gave me my first Lincoln book,
and for Emily Lauren Miller,
part of the new generation of readers

CONTENTS

INTRODUCTION

LINCOLN IN HIS OWN WRITE

Young Abe Lincoln learned to write by reading.

N_O AMERICAN PRESIDENT UNDERSTOOD THE POWER OF WORDS_ better than Abraham Lincoln. Writing, he believed, was "the great invention of the world." And Lincoln became one of the world's great writers.

He lived long before the age of radio and television—long before our leaders could speak to millions of Americans at one time. Lincoln learned to communicate to America through the power of the written word.

We will never know for sure how young Abe Lincoln mastered the skill of self-expression. What we do know is that few masters of the written word ever enjoyed so little training or education. In the "wild region" where he grew up, Lincoln remembered, "there were some schools, so called; but no qualification was ever required of a teacher, beyond *'readin, writin, and cipherin,'* to the Rule of Three. . . . There was absolutely nothing to excite ambition for education. Of course when I came of age I did not know much." He could write "to the Rule of Three"—meaning something like third-grade level—but that was all.

Somehow, Lincoln did learn to express himself with the pen. Actually, he probably did not have the opportunity to use a real pen until he was near adulthood. Pens were for wealthy people, or people who lived in cities. As a youngster growing up in the wilds of Kentucky, Indiana, and Illinois, he might scratch words on the back of a shovel with a rock. He could scrawl in the dirt with a stick, or perhaps find a slate and chalk to use if he happened to be attending a school that had such supplies. If he were fortunate, once in a great while he might even obtain a real pencil. If he did, he would use it until he wore it down to a stump.

Basically, Lincoln learned writing by reading. He read the Bible and *Aesop's Fables* as soon as he was able, and in later years he devoured the poetry of Robert Burns and the plays of William Shakespeare. He was especially fond of one particular life story of his hero, George Washington. "Away back

Lincoln's ability with an ax became legendary during his lifetime.

in my childhood, the earliest days of my being able to read," he recalled many years later, "I got hold of a small book . . . 'Weem's Life of Washington.' I remember all the accounts there given of the battle fields and struggles for the liberties of the country." Between its covers, Lincoln believed, he discovered the origins of the "great promise" that America offered "to all the people of the world to all time to come." Lincoln would echo that promise in his own writings.

Like many future writers of great prose, Abraham Lincoln began by writing rather poor poetry. He wrote poems about his childhood home and about hunting for bears. While still a teenager, he scribbled several amusing rhymes in a practice book. These pages still survive. He probably wrote the verses after a long, hard day of chores: planting seeds, clearing fields, chopping wood, or building log-rail fences. He likely wrote them by the light of the big fire that warmed his parents' log cabin. No one today knows whether he created the rhymes out of his own imagination or copied them from a book. Nevertheless, they are the earliest surviving writings by the sixteenth president of the United States. They show that he wrote not only skillfully but also with a fine, clear penmanship—a rarity in Lincoln's time. They also show that he did not spell especially well. Lincoln boasted excellent handwriting for the rest of his life, but he never did become much of a speller (as you will see).

When he was twenty-two years old, Lincoln left his father's home for good and settled in the village of New Salem, Illinois. There friendly neighbors loaned him useful books about writing and public speaking. One of these volumes was called *A New Guide to the English Tongue,* written by a schoolmaster named Thomas Dilworth. From this book, Lincoln learned the rules of grammar. The book also contained valuable advice about using short words instead of long ones—a rule he would follow for the rest of his life. And the book taught him how to make comparisons, how to structure sentences, and how to pronounce difficult words. "By littles," as Lincoln later put it, he was learning how to write.

Lincoln ran for public office for the first time while still a citizen of New Salem. For this campaign, he prepared his first public speech. It was a complicated and uninspiring bit of writing, and it showed that he still had much to learn about how to express himself clearly. Nonetheless, he won nearly all the votes cast in his village. Lincoln's writing was already brilliant compared to that of his frontier rivals.

Around this time, after deciding that he did not want to spend the rest of his life working as a blacksmith or a surveyor, Lincoln began to study to become a lawyer. Practicing law would teach him more about writing than he ever learned in books. Legal writing required simplicity, truthfulness, and good arguments. His second law partner, an older man named Stephen T. Logan, showed him how to make his legal presentations short, clear, convincing, and to the point. Logan was probably the only teacher of writing Lincoln ever had. Later, by the time Lincoln became the senior partner in his own law firm at the age of thirty-five, he was not only a polished attorney but also a polished writer.

A respected lawyer, Lincoln represented big corporations as well as ordinary people.

For twenty-five years, Lincoln balanced two professions: law and politics. Both required him to write very quickly and very well. Sometimes he had to deliver an argument to a jury by day and a political speech at night. Lincoln wrote all his own legal briefs and political speeches. Often he personally made sure that the speeches were published accurately in the newspapers. After one of his most famous speeches, the Cooper Union Address in New York in 1860 (see page 44), Lincoln went so far as to visit a local newspaper office late at night. There he sat down and personally edited the speech before it was printed. Lincoln had learned much about the power of the written word, and he wanted no mistakes.

The following year, Lincoln became president of the United States. Facing the gravest crisis in the nation's history, he became a greater writer than ever. The Civil War not only tested Lincoln as a leader of men, but it also inspired him as a craftsman of the English language.

Today presidents hire speechwriters and letter writers to help them create their words. Lincoln enjoyed no such assistance. He continued to write all his speeches and important letters himself, using a pen that had to be dipped into an inkwell every few words. There were no computers when Lincoln lived—no typewriters, no photocopying machines, and no carbon paper. Lincoln not only wrote his speeches by hand, but he also often made exact copies on separate sheets of paper when he was finished writing the originals. And he did so without electric lighting, working next to a window during the day and under flickering candles or gas lamps at night.

Nor did words come to Lincoln easily. His law partner remembered, "In the search for words Mr. Lincoln was often at a loss." That was because "in the vast store of words," there were "so few that contained the exact coloring, power, and shape of his ideas." One can only imagine how many hours each day Lincoln devoted to writing. In fact, it is difficult to imagine that he had much time for anything else.

Yet during the darkest days of the Civil War, despite all the terrible responsibilities he faced, Lincoln was able to create some of the most beautiful writing ever crafted by an American. And he did so in an age crowded with great writers of every kind.

One day at the White House, Lincoln was introduced to one such famous author, Harriet Beecher Stowe. Her 1852 novel, *Uncle Tom's Cabin*, had sold the most copies of any book in the century. The book's horrifying picture of the cruelties of slave life had outraged thousands of readers and encouraged them to demand an end to slavery once and for all. Many believed that the book drove the North and South farther apart.

Meeting her that day for the first time, Lincoln gazed down at the tiny woman author and said, "So this is the little lady who made this big war?" The president certainly could appreciate great writing. But so could Harriet Beecher Stowe. Reading the speeches of Abraham Lincoln, she later declared that his words deserved to be "inscribed in letters of gold." She considered him one of the finest writers of his time.

Oddly, Lincoln may never have read *Uncle Tom's Cabin*, the most popular book of his age. He did not like novels and probably never read one, cover to cover, in his life. But when Stowe published a book of facts called

A *Key to Uncle Tom's Cabin,* Lincoln quickly borrowed it from the Library of Congress and read it eagerly. For Abraham Lincoln, great writing had to be real to be important—unless, of course, it was poetry.

For relaxation, President Lincoln read poems and joke books. Often he read them aloud at meetings of his cabinet, much to the disapproval of some of his unsmiling cabinet ministers. Once in a while, he appeared late at night in the bedroom of his private secretaries to recite a funny story he had just found in one of his joke books. He would sit on the bed and laugh along with them, then leave, the tail of his white nightshirt flapping as he closed the door behind him. Such stories eased his great sadness and cleared his mind so that he could resume his own, far more serious writing: official documents, public and personal letters, and occasional speeches. He wrote with special care because he knew that nearly everything he put down on paper might be published in the newspapers. In a way, nearly everything Lincoln wrote as president was designed for two different audiences: the person or group to whom it was addressed and the vast number of Americans who would read it later. Lincoln always saw to it that his best writing was widely published.

Twenty years earlier, when he served in Washington as a congressman, Lincoln made sure that his speeches were printed as pamphlets and mailed back to voters at home in Illinois. Unfortunately, they did not convince the voters to reelect him. He served only a single term as a member of the House of Representatives.

In 1858, when Lincoln was running against Stephen A. Douglas for the U.S. Senate, he challenged his opponent to a series of debates throughout their home state. Although neither man wrote out his speeches in advance, their remarks at the debates were recorded by stenographers. Within days, their words appeared in newspapers throughout the country—one of the first times such prompt reports were possible.

But Lincoln was not satisfied to see the debates printed in newspapers and then forgotten, especially after he lost the election to Douglas. He purchased a huge scrapbook and pasted into it newspaper reports of all seven Lincoln-Douglas debates. Then he convinced a publisher in Columbus, Ohio, to publish the collection as a book. The volume appeared in early 1860, at just the time the Republican Party was meeting in Chicago to choose a candidate for president.

Lincoln was not favored to win that nomination, but he did. Many believe that the appearance of the Lincoln-Douglas debates as a book helped convince delegates to vote for him. It certainly helped introduce his ideas to American voters in the months to come. Lincoln did not campaign for president in 1860; it was considered undignified for presidential candidates to appeal directly to the people for votes. The man who had argued in court-rooms and spoken forcefully at political rallies nearly every day of his adult life slipped out of public view. Once again, his writing spoke for him—and helped send him to the White House.

An artist's view of President Lincoln in the White House, with the U.S. Capitol in the distance.

As president, Lincoln made surprisingly few public appearances. Today the face of Abraham Lincoln is so well-known—staring back at us from coins, stamps, and five-dollar bills—that we assume he spent most of his presidential years among the people. But this was not so. Lincoln believed that presidents belonged in the White House, working for the citizens, not traveling around talking. He gave surprisingly few speeches as president—a total of ninety-five in the four years and one month he served in office. This may seem like a large number, but only seventeen of those speeches were delivered outside the White House. Lincoln did not design his speeches just to be read aloud. He crafted them for publication, too. More often than not, Lincoln spoke to the American people only through his writing.

When the Civil War began, he composed a powerful message to

Congress, declaring, "This is . . . a People's contest." The words were not meant to rally Congress alone. The message was printed throughout the nation and helped convince many northerners that the Union must be preserved.

Many of Lincoln's so-called public letters were published as well. These were letters written to individuals but meant to be read by people everywhere. In one famous example, Lincoln criticized a group of opponents who had complained that northerners were losing too many civil liberties in the government's effort to win the war. Lincoln's powerful response appeared in

Lincoln sits amid the clutter of his White House office in this imaginary rendition of the writing of the Emancipation Proclamation. Inspirational books and pictures are nearby. Lincoln actually wrote some of the famous document across the street at the War Department and some at his summer cottage outside Washington. He composed the first draft in July 1862 and signed the final version nearly six months later.

many newspapers and won widespread praise. On another occasion, Lincoln wrote a letter to his old neighbors in Springfield, Illinois, who objected to the Emancipation Proclamation. "You say you will not fight to free negroes," Lincoln wrote. "Some of them seem willing to fight for you." The letter was read aloud to silence his critics at home and published throughout the nation as well. Once again, Lincoln had used writing to influence the people.

Sometimes even Lincoln's private and personal letters found their way into print. This caused the president much embarrassment. Once, a famous actor of the day sent Lincoln a gift, and the president dashed off a thank-you note in which he described his favorite plays by Shakespeare. The actor was so proud of this letter that he allowed it to be printed in the newspapers. Some newspapers, in turn, teased Lincoln cruelly for his taste in drama. The actor wrote back to apologize, but Lincoln laughed it off. "I have endured a great deal of ridicule . . . ," he declared. "I am used to it." Perhaps that is why he worked so hard on his official writing. He wanted to make sure it could not be criticized.

He spent an especially long time, for example, crafting the Emancipation Proclamation. This was not only his most important act as president but also the most important piece of writing he ever composed. With it, Lincoln proved that the pen was as mighty as the sword. His words would help break the chains that enslaved millions of African Americans. Some have criticized the Emancipation Proclamation because of its dry, uninspiring language. Many critics have complained that Lincoln failed to rise to this great occasion with an unforgettable composition. But Lincoln intentionally wrote the proclamation as a legal document, not a speech. He wanted to make certain that if it were challenged years later in court, it would not be overturned, sending blacks back into slavery. There would be time later to inspire.

It is often forgotten that the Emancipation Proclamation was neither announced at a special ceremony nor read aloud as a speech. Lincoln merely wrote it and signed it, then allowed it to be published in newspaper columns, pamphlets, and handbills throughout the country. It was yet another example of how Lincoln's writing revolutionized America.

Today Lincoln's speeches, letters, messages, telegrams, and notes fill ten books. Some presidents wrote even more, but none wrote as well. And no president before or since has been read as closely or quoted as often as Abraham Lincoln. Perhaps that is the greatest tribute of all.

Lincoln knew that good writing would allow him to speak not only to the people of his own time but to the future as well—to "all distances of time and of space," as he put it. Just as he hoped, his writing continues to speak to us today. It teaches us how words can not only describe history but also change it. His words deserve to be read again and again, because they, too, travel "all distances of time and of space."

What is more, Lincoln's own words tell us much about his inspiring life. They chart the growth of this extraordinary backwoods child as he struggled to master the magic of words and sentences and to find new ideas for a changing world. In a larger sense, his words speak of the possibility that any child, at any time, blessed with talent and devoted to hard work, might someday make the same journey from poverty to the White House.

Most important of all, Lincoln's words not only saved America but also helped create a new America—a country dedicated at last, as Lincoln put it, "to the proposition that all men are created equal."

One of the last photographs of Lincoln.

But Lincoln not only changed American history; he changed American writing as well. Before Lincoln, our leaders spoke in formal, complex sentences cluttered with long words and obscure references to ancient times. Lincoln simplified political writing. He eliminated unnecessary words. He replaced emotion with logic. He made complicated issues clear. He wrote in words everyone could understand—simple words that carried immense power and emotion. "All was clear and exact in his mind," wrote an associate who knew him well. "He was not impulsive, fanciful, or imaginative; but . . . calm and precise." People understood his style and responded to it.

Harriet Beecher Stowe may have created a sensation with her book *Uncle Tom's Cabin*, convincing thousands of Americans that slavery was unjust. But Abraham Lincoln was able to express the same sense of injustice in a single sentence: "He who would *be* no slave, must consent to *have* no slave." Lincoln made certain that the logic of his words became the building blocks of a new America.

On the following pages, those words are brought back to life. They explore every part of Lincoln's public and private life: not only issues of slavery and freedom, war and peace, equality and responsibility, but also work, family, and religion. Together they tell the story of an unforgettable man, in the words of an unforgettable writer. Once again, Lincoln speaks directly to us—in his own voice and "in his own write."

SECTION ONE

THE ILLINOIS YEARS
~ 1825–1860 ~

Lincoln's Kentucky home.

ABRAHAM LINCOLN WAS BORN IN KENTUCKY on February 12, 1809, inside a tiny one-room log cabin with a dirt floor. His father, Thomas, knew how to sign his name—but only "bunglingly," according to the future president. His mother never even learned how to write out the simple words *Nancy Hanks Lincoln*. When her signature was needed, the best she could do was draw an X. Somehow these simple, illiterate parents produced one of the greatest leaders—and greatest writers—America has ever known.

Young Abraham was sent to his first "ABC" school when he was six years old. Such schools were also known as "blab" schools because students there spoke their lessons out loud, often at the same time. Little learning was accomplished. Altogether, Lincoln would spend a total of just one year inside classrooms. Whatever he had "in the way of education," Lincoln later said, he "picked up" along the way—mostly by reading books. Lincoln would later admit that he very much regretted his "want of education." The best he could do was joke about it. One day he was forced to climb through the window of a university to reach a platform where he was to make a speech. "At last," he laughed, "I have gone through college!"

Despite his lack of schooling, the death of his mother, and frequent moves by his father to new neighborhoods in new states, Lincoln developed an amazing gift for expressing himself in words. This talent helped him rise in life from laborer, rail-splitter, flatboat pilot, storekeeper, postmaster, and surveyor to lawyer and political leader. Although his father probably disapproved of Abraham's thirst for knowledge, his new stepmother, Sarah Bush Johnston Lincoln, encouraged him. Young Lincoln surely wanted to spend more time learning than his father thought necessary, and they clashed. They were never close again.

At the age of twenty-two—as soon as he was legally able to do so—Lincoln struck out on his own. Settling in the now-vanished town of New Salem, Illinois, he became extremely popular with friends and neighbors and ran for the state legislature. Even though he won his home district by a vote of 277–7, he lost his first election.

But Lincoln was elected to be the captain of the little company of home-town soldiers that volunteered to fight in the Black Hawk Indian War. He later admitted that no election victory ever gave him more satisfaction. At

New Salem, Illinois, where Lincoln lived as a young man.

home, he became the village postmaster, a job that allowed him to read all the newspapers delivered to the village. He took up storekeeping for a while, but his store failed, and he went deep into debt. Finally, in 1834, he was elected to the state legislature. Lincoln was launched as a politician.

His private life, however, remained unhappy. He was deeply attracted to a village girl named Ann Rutledge, but she died before their relationship could blossom. He next proposed marriage to an older woman named Mary Owens and was shocked when she rejected him.

Reelected and licensed to practice law in 1836, a lonely Lincoln moved to nearby Springfield on April 15, 1837. It was the exact midpoint of his life: he was twenty-eight years old and had twenty-eight more years to live—to the day.

Over the next few years, he grew into an important citizen of the new state capital of Springfield. He became a successful lawyer, won reelection to the legislature, and in 1842 married Mary Todd, daughter of a wealthy banker from Lexington, Kentucky. They had four sons.

The Lincolns spent the next eighteen years in Springfield—that is, Mary and their children remained in town. Lincoln, however, was absent for as much as six months each year in search of legal business in nearby counties. When he wasn't practicing law, he was running for office or helping others to do so.

He also spent two years in Washington as a U.S. congressman, an experience that proved painful both personally and professionally. For one thing, Mary was unable to cope with Washington, and Lincoln sent her west. Even worse, Congressman Lincoln opposed the Mexican War, which made him unpopular back in Springfield. He was not nominated for a second term, although he had agreed in advance not to seek reelection. He returned to Springfield with a bleak political future.

Still, Lincoln had by then grown into an important local figure within his party, the Whigs. They believed that government should invest in roads, bridges, canals, and railroads—"internal improvements," as they were called. They also opposed slavery. Lincoln remained in the Whig Party for most of his political life.

The early 1850s found Lincoln growing prosperous as a lawyer. He began representing railroads and earning large fees. Politics seemed far from his mind. But in 1854, Congress passed a law upsetting the Missouri Compromise, a thirty-four-year-old guarantee that slavery could never exist outside the southern states. Lincoln was "aroused" by this sudden change and reentered the political world.

The only home Lincoln ever owned was in Springfield, Illinois. That home is shown here in the 1860s.

Although he lost an attempt to become a U.S. senator in 1855, then failed in another bid for a Senate seat in 1858, Lincoln became one of the most important and influential antislavery leaders in the country. He helped create and lead the new Republican Party, which argued that slavery should not be allowed to spread into any new territory of the United States. He saw slavery as a moral evil and believed it was poisoning the entire nation. "A house divided against itself cannot stand," Lincoln warned. His unforgettable debates on the slavery issue with Senator Stephen A. Douglas in 1858 propelled him to national fame. Soon thereafter, asked whether he thought himself fit for the White House, Lincoln admitted, "The taste *is* in my mouth a little." But he had never won an office higher than Congress and had won no office at all except the state legislature for more than a decade.

Most people believed that in 1860 the Republican Party would nominate for president a better-known, more experienced leader from the East. But Lincoln had impressed New Yorkers and New Englanders during a speaking tour earlier that year, and when delegates failed to agree on a more famous nominee, the convention chose him. A long and sometimes frustrating career in politics had reached its high point.

That summer, the rival Democratic Party split in half and nominated not one but two men to run for president—one was nominated by the northern wing, the other by the southern wing. Although he probably would have won the election even against one Democrat, the split helped give Lincoln a lopsided electoral victory in November. He won only 40 percent of the popular vote, however. Lincoln would be a minority president.

To make matters worse, news of his election horrified southerners, who were convinced that he meant to take away their slaves. In December, South Carolina seceded from the United States. And by the time Lincoln was ready to leave for Washington for his inauguration, Mississippi, Florida, Alabama, Georgia, and Louisiana had followed South Carolina out of the Union. Lincoln faced an unhappy choice: either consent to lead half the country or go to war to bring the southern states back. No man ever entered the White House amid a more serious national emergency.

In the pages that follow—in speeches, letters, and other writings—Abraham Lincoln grows from prairie politician to president-elect. He discusses slavery, government, and law. He wrote private letters to family and friends in the same earnest style he used for his speeches.

A popular campaign song of the day suggested that "Old Abe Lincoln Came Out of the Wilderness"—hinting that he suddenly appeared on the national scene as if by magic. In truth, Lincoln's path to greatness was slow and difficult. But the power of his words was clear from the start, and eventually it was his words and ideas that carried him to the White House.

—————▷◦◁—————

RHYMES FROM HIS PRACTICE BOOK- 1825

Lincoln wrote these poems when he was around sixteen years old. They were discovered on the pages of an old arithmetic book in which he practiced addition and multiplication. Two of the rhymes are funny, the other sad—very much like Lincoln himself, who loved to laugh but often grew melancholy. Apparently, young Lincoln was still unsure about his spelling. He clearly had much to learn. These are the earliest known examples of his writing.

Abraham Lincoln
his hand and pen
he will be good but
god knows When

———◄►———

Time What an emty vaper
tis and days how swift they are swift as an indian arr[ow]
fly on like a shooting star the presant moment Just [is here]
then slides away in h[as]te that we [can] never say they['re ours]
but [only say] th[ey]'re past

———◄►———

Abraham Lincoln is my nam[e]
And with my pen I wrote the same
I wrote in both hast and speed
and left it here for fools to read

Boyhood of Lincoln was painted by Eastman Johnson in 1868.
Johnson was an American artist who lived from 1824 to 1906.

Springfield, Illinois, in about the 1850s.

PROTESTING SLAVERY-MARCH 3, 1837
Resolution Before the Illinois State Legislature

In 1837, Democrats in the Illinois legislature introduced a resolution criticizing abolitionists, who wished to outlaw slavery immediately. Lincoln and a fellow Whig, Dan Stone, fought back with a resolution of their own. It criticized abolitionists much less harshly than the first resolution and criticized slavery severely. It was Lincoln's first public protest against slavery.

The following protest was presented to the House, which was read and ordered to be spread on the journals, to wit:

"Resolutions upon the subject of domestic slavery having passed both branches of the General Assembly at its present session, the undersigned hereby protest against the passage of the same.

They believe that the institution of slavery is founded on both injustice and bad policy; but that the promulgation of abolition doctrines tends rather to increase than to abate its evils.

They believe that the Congress of the United States has no

power, under the constitution, to interfere with the institution of slavery in the different States.

They believe that the Congress of the United States has the power, under the constitution, to abolish slavery in the District of Columbia; but that that power ought not to be exercised unless at the request of the people of said District.

The difference between these opinions and those contained in the said resolutions, is their reason for entering this protest."

DAN STONE,
A. LINCOLN,
Representatives from the county of Sangamon.

⊰◆⊱

FROM "MY CHILDHOOD-HOME I SEE AGAIN" FEBRUARY [?] 1846

Lincoln wrote this long, sentimental poem about his prairie origins after visiting his boyhood home in Indiana. He felt "a little poetic" and composed these verses. The poem showed that Lincoln had mixed feelings about his upbringing. He remembered things that were "gross and vile," but he also recalled "enchanted" scenes "bathed in liquid light."

Lincoln the Rail Splitter.

My childhood-home I see again,
    And gladden with the view;
And still as mem'ries crowd my brain,
    There's sadness in it too.

O memory! thou mid-way world
    'Twixt Earth and Paradise,
Where things decayed, and loved ones lost
    In dreamy shadows rise.

And freed from all that's gross or vile,
    Seem hallowed, pure, and bright,
Like scenes in some enchanted isle,
    All bathed in liquid light.

As distant mountains please the eye,
    When twilight chases day —
As bugle-tones, that, passing by,
    In distance die away —

As leaving some grand water-fall
    We ling'ring, list it's roar,
So memory will hallow all
    We've known, but know no more.

Now twenty years have passed away,
    Since here I bid farewell
To woods, and fields, and scenes of play
    And school-mates loved so well.

Where many were, how few remain
    Of old familiar things!
But seeing these to mind again
    The lost and absent brings.

The friends I left that parting day —
    How changed, as time has sped!
Young childhood grown, strong manhood grey,
    And half of all are dead.

LONELY CONGRESSMAN MISSES HIS FAMILY
APRIL 16, 1848
Letter to Mary Lincoln

When Lincoln first went to Washington as a member of Congress from Illinois, Mary and their sons Robert and Edward went with him. But the family did not thrive in Washington, and Mary eventually took the boys home to her father's house in Lexington, Kentucky. Evidently, Mary was miserable there, too. Although her letter to her husband is lost, his gentle reply, reprinted here, hints that the Lincolns were unhappy when they were together but also unhappy when apart.

Mary Lincoln in about 1846, a few years after her marriage to Abraham Lincoln.

Dear Mary:

In this troublesome world, we are never quite satisfied. When you were here, I thought you hindered me some in attending to business; but now, having nothing but business— no variety—it has grown exceedingly tasteless to me. I hate to sit down and direct documents, and I hate to stay in this old room by myself. You know I told you in last sunday's letter, I was going to make a little speech during the week; but the week has passed away without my getting a chance to do so; and now my interest in the subject has passed away too. Your second and third letters have been received since I wrote before. Dear Eddy thinks father is *"gone tapila[.]"* Has any further discovery been made as to the breaking into your grand-mother's house? If I were she, I would not remain there alone. You mention that your uncle John Parker is likely to be at Lexington. Dont forget to present him my very kindest regards.

I went yesterday to hunt the little plaid stockings, as you wished; but found that McKnight has quit business, and Allen had not a single pair of the description you give, and only one plaid pair of any sort that I thought would fit "Eddy's dear little feet." I have a notion to make another trial to-morrow morning. If I could get them, I have an excellent chance of sending them. Mr. Warrick Tunstall, of St. Louis is here. He is to leave early this week, and to go by Lexington. He says he knows you, and will call to see you; and he voluntarily asked, if I had not some package to send to you.

I wish you to enjoy yourself in every possible way; but is there no danger of wounding the feelings of your good father, by being so openly intimate with the Wickliffe family?

Mrs. Broome has not removed yet; but she thinks of doing so to-morrow. All the house—or rather, all with whom you were on decided good terms—send their love to you. The others say nothing.

Very soon after you went away, I got what I think a very pretty set of shirt-bosom studs—modest little ones, jet, set in gold, only costing 50 cents a piece, or 1.50 for the whole.

Suppose you do not prefix the "Hon" to the address on your letters to me any more. I like the letters very much, but I would rather they should not have that upon them. It is not necessary, as I suppose you have thought, to have them to come free.

And you are entirely free from head-ache? That is good—good—considering it is the first spring you have been free from it since we were acquainted. I am afraid you will get so well, and fat, and young, as to be wanting to marry again. Tell Louisa I want her to watch you a little for me. Get weighed, and write me how much you weigh.

I did not get rid of the impression of that foolish dream about dear Bobby till I got your letter written the same day.

What did he and Eddy think of the little letters father sent them? Dont let the blessed fellows forget father.

A day or two ago Mr. Strong, here in Congress, said to me that Matilda would visit here within two or three weeks. Suppose you write her a letter, and enclose it in one of mine; and if she comes I will deliver it to her, and if she does not, I will send it to her. Most affectionately

A. LINCOLN

Lincoln in about 1846, the year he was elected to the U.S. Congress.

HOW TO BE A GOOD LAWYER - JULY 1, 1850 [?]
Notes for a Lecture on the Law

Lincoln prepared these remarks for a speech on the practice of law, but there is no record that he ever delivered such a lecture. Still, the notes reveal a great deal about Lincoln's views on the life and work of an attorney. He practiced law for twenty-five years.

I am not an accomplished lawyer. I find quite as much material for a lecture in those points wherein I have failed, as in those wherein I have been moderately successful. The leading rule for the lawyer, as for the man of every other calling, is diligence. Leave nothing for to-morrow which can be done to-day. Never let your correspondence fall behind. Whatever piece of business you have in hand, before stopping, do all the labor pertaining to it which can then be done. When you bring a common-law suit, if you have the facts for doing so, write the declaration at once. If a law point be involved, examine the books, and note the authority you rely on upon the declaration itself, where you are sure to find it when wanted. The same of defenses and pleas. In business not likely to be litigated,—ordinary collection cases, foreclosures, partitions, and the like,—make all examinations of titles, and note them, and even draft orders and decrees in advance. This course has a triple advantage; it avoids omissions and neglect, saves your labor when once done, performs the labor out of court when you have leisure, rather than in court when you have not. Extemporaneous speaking should be practised and cultivated. It is the lawyer's avenue to the public. However able and faithful he may be in other respects, people are slow to bring him business if he cannot make a speech. And yet there is not a more fatal error to young lawyers than relying too much on speech-making. If any one, upon his rare powers of speaking, shall claim an exemption from the drudgery of the law, his case is a failure in advance.

Discourage litigation. Persuade your neighbors to compromise whenever you can. Point out to them how the nominal winner is often a real loser—in fees, expenses, and waste of time. As a peacemaker the lawyer has a superior opportunity of being a good man. There will still be business enough.

Never stir up litigation. A worse man can scarcely be found than one who does this. Who can be more nearly a fiend than he who habitually overhauls the register of deeds in search of defects in titles, whereon to stir up strife, and put money in his pocket? A moral tone ought to be infused into the profession which should drive such men out of it.

The matter of fees is important, far beyond the mere question of bread and butter involved. Properly attended to, fuller justice is done to both lawyer and client. An exorbitant fee should never be claimed. As a general rule never take your

A print of Lincoln during his most famous court case, in which he defended young Duff Armstrong, who was charged with murder. The artist added Lincoln's beard. In truth, he was clean shaven during the Armstrong trial.

whole fee in advance, nor any more than a small retainer. When fully paid beforehand, you are more than a common mortal if you can feel the same interest in the case, as if something was still in prospect for you, as well as for your client. And when you lack interest in the case the job will very likely lack skill and diligence in the performance. Settle the amount of fee and take a note in advance. Then you will feel that you are working for something, and you are sure to do your work faithfully and well. Never sell a fee note—at least not before the consideration service is performed. It leads to negligence and dishonesty—negligence by losing interest in the case, and dishonesty in refusing to refund when you have allowed the consideration to fail.

There is a vague popular belief that lawyers are necessarily dishonest. I say vague, because when we consider to what extent confidence and honors are reposed in and conferred upon lawyers by the people, it appears improbable that their impression of dishonesty is very distinct and vivid. Yet the impression is common, almost universal. Let no young man choosing the law for a calling for a moment yield to the popular belief—resolve to be honest at all events; and if in your own judgment you cannot be an honest lawyer, resolve to be honest without being a lawyer. Choose some other occupation, rather than one in the choosing of which you do, in advance, consent to be a knave.

Refusing to Visit His Dying Father
January 12, 1851
Letter to John D. Johnston

Lincoln's relationship with his father was not good. In January 1851, he received word that old Thomas Lincoln was dying and wanted very much to see him one last time. Abraham refused to go. Thomas died without speaking to his son.

Sarah Bush Johnston Lincoln, Abraham Lincoln's stepmother (left), and Thomas Lincoln, his father (right).

Dear Brother:

On the day before yesterday I received a letter from Harriett, written at Greenup. She says she has just returned from your house; and that Father [is very] low, and will hardly recover. She also s[ays] you have written me two letters; and that [although] you do not expect me to come now, yo[u wonder] that I do not write. I received both your [letters, and] although I have not answered them, it is no[t because] I have forgotten them, or been uninterested about them—but because it appeared to me I could write nothing which could do any good. You already know I desire that neither Father or Mother shall be in want of any comfort either in health or sickness while they live; and I feel sure you have not failed to use my name, if necessary, to procure a doctor, or any thing else for

Father in his present sickness. My business is such that I could hardly leave home now, if it were not, as it is, that my own wife is sick-abed. (It is a case of baby-sickness, and I suppose is not dangerous.) I sincerely hope Father may yet recover his health; but at all events tell him to remember to call upon, and confide in, our great, and good, and merciful Maker; who will not turn away from him in any extremity. He notes the fall of a sparrow, and numbers the hairs of our heads; and He will not forget the dying man, who puts his trust in Him. Say to him that if we could meet now, it is doubtful whether it would not be more painful than pleasant; but that if it be his lot to go now, he will soon have a joyous [meeting] with many loved ones gone before; and where [the rest] of us, through the help of God, hope ere-long [to join] them.

Write me again when you receive this. Affectionately

A. LINCOLN

WHAT GOVERNMENT SHOULD DO-JULY 1, 1854 [?]
Fragment on the Role of Government

We do not know for sure when Lincoln made these notes about what government ought to do for its people. Most experts date the notes 1854, when he reentered politics. This statement is still quoted by politicians today.

The legitimate object of government is "to do for the people what needs to be done, but which they can not, by individual effort, do at all, or do so well, for themselves." There are many such things—some of them exist independently of the injustice in the world. Making and maintaining roads, bridges, and the like; providing for the helpless young and afflicted; common schools; and disposing of deceased men's property, are instances.

But a far larger class of objects springs from the injustice of

Lincoln in 1854.

men. If one people will make war upon another, it is a necessity with that other to unite and cooperate for defense. Hence the military department. If some men will kill, or beat, or constrain others, or despoil them of property, by force, fraud, or noncompliance with contracts, it is a common object with peaceful and just men to prevent it. Hence the criminal and civil departments.

━━◆━━

FROM A SPEECH ON THE DRED SCOTT DECISION
JUNE 26, 1857
Springfield, Illinois

The Supreme Court's Dred Scott decision angered Lincoln. It held that blacks could never be American citizens and that slaves were no better than property anywhere in the country, North as well as South. Lincoln was not quite ready to embrace full racial equality, but he was fully prepared to argue for equal opportunity. He delivered this stinging attack at the state capitol.

Now I protest against that counterfeit logic which concludes that, because I do not want a black woman for a *slave* I must necessarily want her for a *wife*. I need not have her for either, I can just leave her alone. In some respects she certainly is not my equal; but in her natural right to eat the bread she earns with her own hands without asking leave of any one else, she is my equal, and the equal of all others.

Lincoln posed for photographer Alexander Hesler in 1857, the year before he ran for the U.S. Senate.

FROM THE "HOUSE DIVIDED" SPEECH—JUNE 16, 1858
Springfield, Illinois

Borrowing a phrase from the Bible—"a house divided against itself cannot stand"—Lincoln gave this unforgettable speech to the Republican Party convention that nominated him to run for the Senate. The speech no doubt shocked many of his listeners. After all, Lincoln was predicting that America could no longer exist half slave and half free. For years, Lincoln tried to play down the warning he issued in the address. He was much more cautious in the future. But the speech stirred the state and the nation, and it helped make Lincoln famous outside Illinois. This is the opening section of that extraordinary speech.

The Old State Capitol in Springfield, Illinois.

Mr. PRESIDENT and Gentlemen of the Convention.

If we could first know *where* we are, and *whither* we are tending, we could then better judge *what* to do, and *how* to do it.

We are now far into the *fifth* year, since a policy was initiated, with the *avowed* object, and *confident* promise, of putting an end to slavery agitation.

Under the operation of that policy, that agitation has not only, *not ceased*, but has *constantly augmented*.

In *my* opinion, it *will* not cease, until a *crisis* shall have been reached, and passed.

"A house divided against itself cannot stand."

I believe this government cannot endure, permanently half *slave* and half *free*.

I do not expect the Union to be *dissolved*—I do not expect the house to *fall*—but I *do* expect it will cease to be divided.

It will become *all* one thing, or *all* the other.

Either the *opponents* of slavery, will arrest the further spread of it, and place it where the public mind shall rest in the belief that it is in course of ultimate extinction; or its *advocates* will push it forward, till it shall become alike lawful in *all* the States, *old* as well as *new*—*North* as well as *South*.

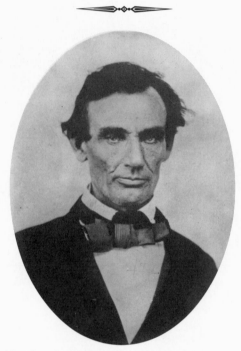

Lincoln a few days before his fifth debate with
Stephen A. Douglas in Galesburg, Illinois.

HIS IDEA OF DEMOCRACY-AUGUST 1, 1858 [?]

Lincoln never said these words publicly, but they later became famous when printed in biographies and history books. He may have prepared the statement for use in his 1858 campaign against Senator Douglas. If so, he never used them.

As I would not be a *slave*, so I would not be a *master*. This expresses my idea of democracy. Whatever differs from this, to the extent of the difference, is no democracy.

The Robert Marshall Root painting of the fourth Lincoln-Douglas debate in Charleston, Illinois. Douglas is sitting to the left of Lincoln.

EXCERPTS FROM THE LINCOLN-DOUGLAS DEBATES AUGUST–OCTOBER 1858

The Lincoln-Douglas debates became, and remain today, the most famous political debates ever held in America. At the time, they attracted crowds as large as twenty thousand people. But their real fame came when the candidates' speeches were reprinted in newspapers throughout the country and later published in a book.

Throughout the summer and fall of 1858, the tall, gangly Lincoln and the short, stout Douglas argued the slavery issue in open fields, town squares, and county fairgrounds. They spoke in both blistering heat and chilling winds. They met in areas where most people supported Lincoln and in areas where most supported Douglas. But wherever they went, their debates became huge events. People came from nearby towns to hear the two politicians, bringing picnic lunches and arguing with their neighbors about which candidate was better. Brass bands played to entertain the crowd before each debate. Each event became a festival.

The speeches themselves took three hours. The first candidate spoke for an hour, the second for an hour and a half, and then the first returned for a final half hour. Politics was considered entertainment in the 1850s. Audiences loved long, exciting speeches and frequently interrupted the speakers to cheer or ridicule them.

Douglas won reelection that year, but Lincoln would have triumphed had the voters been able to cast their votes directly for one man or the other. In 1858, however, citizens voted for state legislators, who in turn elected that state's U.S. senators. Since more Democratic state legislators were elected in Illinois, Douglas was chosen senator. The system was not changed until the twentieth century.

Following are some excerpts from Lincoln's speeches at some of the debates, which were held at Ottawa on August 21, Freeport on August 27, Jonesboro on September 15, Charleston on September 18, Galesburg on October 7, Quincy on October 13, and Alton on October 15. The remarks were recorded by a stenographer writing in shorthand, then the notes were edited by pro-Republican newspapermen and later by Lincoln himself. These are the versions that appeared in the book of the debates two years later. The words probably sound far better than the speeches Lincoln actually delivered without written texts during the debates themselves. But they show how Lincoln wanted us to remember what he said during that exciting campaign of 1858.

Readers will realize that what set Lincoln apart was his strong belief that slavery was morally wrong.

Notice that Lincoln referred to his opponent as "Judge" instead of "Senator" to annoy him. Douglas had been a judge many years before.

FROM LINCOLN'S SPEECH
AT THE FIRST DEBATE
AUGUST 21, 1858
Ottawa, Illinois

Henry Clay once said of a class of men who would repress all tendencies to liberty and ultimate emancipation, that they must, if they would do this, go back to the era of our Independence, and muzzle the cannon which thunders its annual joyous return; they must blow out the moral lights around us; they must penetrate the human soul, and eradicate there the love of liberty; and then and not till then, could they perpetuate slavery in this country! [Loud cheers.] To my thinking, Judge Douglas is, by his example and vast influence, doing that very thing in this community, [cheers,] when he says that the negro has nothing in the Declaration of Independence. Henry Clay plainly understood the contrary. Judge Douglas is going back to the era of our Revolution, and to the extent of his ability, muzzling the cannon which thunders its annual joyous return. When he invites any people willing to have slavery, to establish it, he is blowing out the moral lights around us. [Cheers.] When he says he "cares not whether slavery is voted down or voted up," —that it is a sacred right of self government—he is in my judgment penetrating the human soul and eradicating the light of reason and the love of liberty in this American people. [Enthusiastic and continued applause.]

———⟫◆⟪———

FROM LINCOLN'S SPEECH AT THE THIRD DEBATE SEPTEMBER 15, 1858
Jonesboro, Illinois

While I am upon this subject, I will make some answers briefly to certain propositions that Judge Douglas has put. He says, "Why can't this Union endure permanently, half slave and half free?" I have said that I supposed it could not, and I will try, before this new audience, to give briefly some of the reasons for entertaining that opinion. Another form of his question is, "Why can't we let it stand as our fathers placed it?" That is the exact difficulty between us, I say that Judge Douglas and his friends have changed them from the position in which our fathers originally placed it. I say in the way our fathers originally left the slavery question, the institution was in the course of ultimate extinction, and the public mind rested in the belief that it *was* in the course of ultimate extinction. I say when this government was first established it was the policy of its founders to prohibit the spread of slavery into the new Territories of the United States, where it had not existed. But Judge Douglas and his friends have broken up that policy and placed it upon a new basis by which it is to become national and perpetual. All I have asked or desired anywhere is that it should be placed back again upon the basis that the fathers of our government originally placed it upon. I have no doubt that it *would* become extinct, for all time to come, if we but re-adopted the policy of the fathers by restricting it to the limits it has already covered—restricting it from the new Territories.

FROM LINCOLN'S SPEECH AT THE FOURTH DEBATE SEPTEMBER 18, 1858
Charleston, Illinois

The other way is for us to surrender and let Judge Douglas and his friends have their way and plant slavery over all the States—cease speaking of it as in any way a wrong—regard slavery as one of the common matters of property, and speak of negroes as we do of our horses and cattle. But while it drives on in its state of progress as it is now driving, and as it has driven for the last five years, I have ventured the opinion, and I say to-day, that we will have no end to the slavery agitation until it takes one turn or the other. [Applause.] I do not mean that when it takes a turn towards ultimate extinction it will be in a day, nor in a year, nor in two years. I do not suppose that in the most peaceful way ultimate extinction would occur in less than a hundred years at the least; but that it will occur in the best way for both races in God's own good time, I have no doubt. [Applause.]

FROM LINCOLN'S SPEECH AT THE FIFTH DEBATE OCTOBER 7, 1858
Galesburg, Illinois

Now, I confess myself as belonging to that class in the country who contemplate slavery as a moral, social and political evil, having due regard for its actual existence amongst us and the difficulties of getting rid of it in any satisfactory way, and to all the constitutional obligations which have been thrown about it; but, nevertheless, desire a policy that looks to the prevention of it as a wrong, and looks hopefully to the time when as a wrong it may come to an end. [Great applause.]

———>◆<———

FROM LINCOLN'S SPEECH AT THE SEVENTH DEBATE OCTOBER 15, 1858
Alton, Illinois

That [slavery] is the issue that will continue in this country when these poor tongues of Judge Douglas and myself shall be silent. It is the eternal struggle between these two principles—right and wrong—throughout the world. They are the two principles that have stood face to face from the beginning of time; and will ever continue to struggle. The one is the common right of humanity and the other the divine right of kings. It is the same principle in whatever shape it develops itself. It is the same spirit that says, "You work and toil and earn bread, and I'll eat it." [Loud applause.] No matter in what shape it comes, whether from the mouth of a king who seeks to bestride the people of his own nation and live by the fruit of their labor, or from one race of men as an apology for enslaving another race, it is the same tyrannical principle.

———>◆<———

FROM HIS COOPER UNION ADDRESS
FEBRUARY 27, 1860
New York City

Invited to give a speech in Brooklyn, New York, Lincoln arrived to learn that so many tickets had been sold that the event had to be moved to a larger auditorium. And so the Republican leader from the West gave his first speech in the East at Cooper Union, a college in Manhattan. The speech caused a sensation. One newspaper wrote that no man had ever made a better first impression on a New York audience. By the time Lincoln returned home, eastern Republicans were beginning to speak of him as a future president of the United States.

Wrong as we think slavery is, we can yet afford to let it alone where it is, because that much is due to the necessity arising from its actual presence in the nation; but can we, while our votes will prevent it, allow it to spread into the National Territories, and to overrun us here in these Free States? If our sense of duty forbids this, then let us stand by our duty, fearlessly and effectively. Let us be diverted by none of those sophistical contrivances wherewith we are so industriously plied and belabored—contrivances such as groping for some middle ground between the right and the wrong, vain as the search for a man who should be neither a living man nor a dead man—such as a policy of "don't care" on a question about which all true men do care—such as Union appeals beseeching true Union men to yield to Disunionists, reversing the divine rule, and calling, not the sinners, but the righteous to repentance—such as invocations to Washington, imploring men to unsay what Washington said, and undo what Washington did.

Neither let us be slandered from our duty by false accusations against us, nor frightened from it by menaces of destruction to the Government nor of dungeons to ourselves. LET US HAVE FAITH THAT RIGHT MAKES MIGHT, AND IN THAT FAITH, LET US, TO THE END, DARE TO DO OUR DUTY AS WE UNDERSTAND IT.

Photographer Mathew Brady took this picture of Lincoln the day
he delivered his Cooper Union Address in New York City.

<hr />

ACCEPTING THE NOMINATION FOR PRESIDENT
MAY 19, 1860
Springfield, Illinois

Lincoln did not attend the Republican National Convention that
nominated him for president on May 18, 1860. The following day, a delega-
tion came down to Springfield from Chicago, where the convention was
held, to notify Lincoln "officially" of the news he had already received by
telegraph. These are the remarks he gave in gratitude for the nomination.

Mr. Chairman and gentlemen of the committee, I tender [to] you, and through you [to] the Republican National Convention, and all the people represented in it, my profoundest thanks for the high honor done me, which you now formally announce. Deeply, and even painfully sensible of the great responsibility which is inseparable from that [this high] honor—a responsibility which I could almost wish had fallen upon some one of the far more eminent men and experienced statesmen whose distinguished names were before the Convention, I shall, by your leave, consider more fully the resolutions of the Convention, denominated the platform, and without unseasonable [unnecessary or unreasonable] delay, respond to you, Mr. Chairman, in writing—not doubting now, that the platform will be found satisfactory, and the nomination [gratefully] accepted.

And now, I will not longer defer the pleasure of taking you, and each of you, by the hand.

President-elect Abraham Lincoln in late 1860, with the beginnings of a beard.

SECTION TWO

THE WHITE HOUSE YEARS
⟿ 1861–1865 ⟿

The White House, 1861-1865.

"*I CLAIM NOT TO HAVE CONTROLLED EVENTS*," Abraham Lincoln declared in the midst of the bloody Civil War, "but confess plainly that events have controlled me."

Lincoln was being modest. By the time he wrote those words, hundreds of thousands of American soldiers had sacrificed their lives—either to save the Union or to destroy it. What was more, Lincoln's Emancipation Proclamation had begun freeing millions of African Americans from slavery. And his Gettysburg Address had offered Americans a vision of America under what he called "a new birth of freedom." It is not surprising that many people referred to the bloody rebellion as "Mr. Lincoln's war."

As president, Abraham Lincoln liked to tell people that he was merely swept along by events. In truth, he provided the strong leadership and stirring words that were required to save American democracy and to include African Americans within its blessings. Lincoln came much closer to the truth when he told Congress in 1862, "We cannot escape history." Lincoln came face to face with history once he entered the White House, and he did not escape it. Instead, he *made* history—with deeds and words alike.

The day before his fifty-second birthday in February 1861, Lincoln began a long, slow train journey to Washington for his inauguration. He faced a task, he told his neighbors, "greater than that which rested upon Washington." Lincoln was sworn into office on March 4, with soldiers guarding him carefully against threats of violence. The next month, South Carolina troops opened fire on Fort Sumter, a U.S. garrison located in Charleston harbor, in southern territory. The Civil War was officially under way.

Over the next four years, organized into the Confederate States of America, the South fought for the right to leave the Union. The Confederacy compared its struggle to the fight for freedom from England during the American Revolution. In truth, the Civil War was mostly about slavery. Southerners wanted to keep their slaves and extend slavery to the new territories of the country. Northerners like Lincoln demanded that slavery not be allowed to spread anywhere. And, as Lincoln later put it, "the war came."

Lincoln insisted that no state had the right to leave the United States merely because it disagreed with the results of an election. "Ballots," Lincoln declared, were more powerful than "bullets." He believed that the bond that tied the Union together was sacred. He was willing to fight to save it. The result was the deadliest war in American history.

At first, most northerners, including Lincoln, believed that the war would be a brief one. The North boasted many more people and far greater manufacturing might. But when Confederate forces unexpectedly defeated Union troops at the Battle of Bull Run, Virginia, in July 1861, both sides prepared for a long contest. The war dragged on, and many soldiers died of wounds or disease. Lincoln ordered the Union navy to blockade southern ports, cutting off supplies. As a result, southerners slowly ran out of food, clothing, and medicine. Many Confederates blamed Lincoln for the shortages that caused great hunger and suffering throughout the South.

In some ways, the war made Lincoln as stern with northerners as he was with southerners. Worried about spies and political opponents who encouraged citizens in the North to oppose the war, Lincoln took on special powers that no president had assumed before. He canceled the right to speedy trials for critics who were suspected of being traitors. He allowed others to be arrested and held in military prisons without being formally charged with crimes. And he permitted some northern newspapers to be closed down if they criticized the war effort too harshly.

Many worried northerners charged that Lincoln's actions were unnecessary and unconstitutional. Lincoln replied that he was allowed to take such actions as long as America faced an emergency that threatened to destroy the country. He was sorry that some civil liberties had to be taken away temporarily, but, he explained, any good doctor would cut off a wounded man's leg to save the patient's life. To allow traitors to wreck the Union would be like killing the patient to save his leg. Some critics called Lincoln a dictator, but his admirers continued to refer to him fondly as "Uncle Abe" or "Father Abraham."

Despite Lincoln's extraordinary efforts to save the Union, northern military forces did not win an important eastern victory until the Battle of Antietam in September 1862. Five days later, Lincoln issued the Emancipation Proclamation. It was the greatest act of his presidency. The proclamation declared that unless rebel states returned to the Union within 100 days, all their slaves would be "forever free."

Some modern historians have suggested that the proclamation did little to free the slaves. It did not, after all, free slaves in southern states that remained in the Union, such as Delaware and Maryland. Some critics have even questioned Lincoln's personal belief in liberty. But Lincoln deserves to be remembered as the "Great Emancipator." He did what no leader had been bold enough to do: strike a fatal blow against slavery and begin its permanent destruction.

If anything, at first the Emancipation Proclamation hurt the Union war effort. Many soldiers who had been willing to fight to save the country were not so willing to fight to free African American slaves. In December 1862, just three months after the proclamation was announced, Union troops were badly beaten at the Battle of Fredericksburg, Virginia. For Lincoln and the Union, it was one of the worst defeats of the war. But on January 1, 1863, Lincoln fulfilled his promise to America and signed his final Emancipation Proclamation. Slaves in the Confederacy were declared free. Union soldiers were encouraged to liberate them wherever they marched. And for the first time, African Americans were allowed to join the Union army and fight for their own freedom.

Eventually, Union forces won major victories in the West, opening the vital Mississippi River. Then in July 1863, Lincoln's armies won twin triumphs at Vicksburg, Mississippi, and Gettysburg, Pennsylvania. It seemed to be a major turning point for the North, but by mid-1864 things were again looking bleak. Nevertheless, Lincoln decided to seek a second term as president.

No country in the midst of a civil war had ever allowed a national election to go on as scheduled. But Lincoln believed that if the election were postponed, the Union cause would suffer a huge moral defeat. "The election," he said, was "a necessity." "We can not have free government without elections," he explained. For many months, Lincoln was convinced that he would be defeated. But when Union armies took Atlanta, his political fortunes improved. He went on to win a major victory in November, capturing

In this 1865 print, *Abraham Lincoln's Last Reception,* Abraham and Mary Lincoln greet Union generals, cabinet members, and others in the East Room of the White House.

55 percent of the votes. Of course, only the loyal states voted in 1864. Had the Confederate states cast ballots, the results would have been quite different. But to Lincoln, the election showed "how *strong* we still are."

In his early political career in Illinois, Lincoln gave hundreds of speeches and made countless other public appearances. As president and commander in chief, however, he seldom appeared before the people. Nor did he campaign for reelection. He preferred to let his writing campaign for him. More than ever, Lincoln's words became valuable weapons in the war for freedom and Union. As he prepared to become the first president since

Andrew Jackson to be elected to two terms, he struggled with some of the most important words he would ever write: an inaugural address that would not only explain the long war but also hold out the hope of a speedy peace.

In 1862, Lincoln's middle son, Willie, died at the age of eleven. His death sent Mary Lincoln into a deep mental depression from which she never completely recovered. Lincoln mourned, too. In fact, throughout the war, Lincoln's personal tragedies made his difficult job as president even harder to bear. The loss of his son, and the loss of so many other fathers' sons in battle, weighed heavily on his heart. Photographs show that within four years, Lincoln aged from a young to an old man.

His determination was finally rewarded. In the spring of 1865, after months of bloody fighting in Virginia, Confederate forces finally surrendered. The long Civil War was over. States began approving a new constitutional amendment ending slavery everywhere. Lincoln's brilliant second inaugural address, delivered on March 4, 1865, pleaded for "malice toward none" and "charity for all."

But before he could enjoy the return of peace, Lincoln became a victim of the war. While sitting in a theater on Good Friday, April 14, 1865, he was shot in the head by John Wilkes Booth, a famous actor who believed passionately in slavery and the Confederacy. Lincoln died of his wounds the next morning.

President Lincoln's box inside Ford's Theatre, where he sat on the evening of April 14, 1865.

President Lincoln's railroad funeral car.

Lincoln's body was taken home to Illinois along the same route the living Lincoln had traveled from Illinois to Washington four years earlier. All along the way, admirers gathered by the thousands to pay tribute to the man they now called the "Savior of the Union" and the "Martyr of Liberty."

Throughout the North, Americans mourned Lincoln. They praised him in their churches, hung his picture on the walls of their homes, and reread the words he had written during the Civil War. Much criticized during his life, he was recognized in death as one of our greatest leaders and most inspiring writers.

On the pages that follow, we remember how Lincoln used words to wage war and rebuild America. He offered hope during the darkest hours of the Civil War, lifting the nation's spirits with the sheer power of his writing. And when victory finally came, he generously asked not for punishment but for peace and prosperity.

Throughout the war, Lincoln wrote not only the words he read in public but also anxious letters to his generals, generous pardons for soldiers condemned to death, and warm letters to his wife and sons. He took time to write a rhyme or repeat a remark he thought particularly amusing. He crafted proclamations and messages, clever letters to newspaper editors, and letters of condolence to the parents and children of dead war heroes. He wrote for men and women, adults and children, whites and blacks, and, on one occasion, Native Americans. He even paused to write a prayer about the will of God. Above all, however, he composed speeches. Lincoln's beautiful speeches have become part of American literature.

At one point in his most famous speech, the Gettysburg Address, Lincoln sounded far too modest. "The world will little note, nor long remember what we say here," he declared. But he was wrong. The world has remembered what Lincoln said at Gettysburg, as well as what he said and wrote throughout his White House years.

Farewell Address – February 11, 1861
Springfield, Illinois

On a cold and rainy winter morning, Abraham Lincoln boarded a train in Springfield to begin his long journey to Washington to become president. It was the day before his fifty-second birthday, and he wore a new beard that completely changed his appearance. With his neighbors standing silently before him, Lincoln stood at the back of the train and said his final good-bye with this beautiful speech. He would never see his hometown again.

My friends—No one, not in my situation, can appreciate my feeling of sadness at this parting. To this place, and the kindness of these people, I owe every thing. Here I have lived a quarter of a century, and have passed from a young to an old man. Here my children have been born, and one is buried. I now leave, not knowing when, or whether ever, I may return, with a task before me greater than that which rested upon Washington. Without the assistance of that Divine Being, who ever attended him, I cannot succeed. With that assistance I cannot fail. Trusting in Him, who can go with me, and remain with you and be every where for good, let us confidently hope that all will yet be well. To His care commending you, as I hope in your prayers you will commend me, I bid you an affectionate farewell[.]

Lincoln's long journey from Springfield, Illinois, to Washington, D.C., began at the Springfield railroad depot in February 1861.

SPEECH IN INDEPENDENCE HALL - FEBRUARY 22, 1861
Philadelphia, Pennsylvania

As luck would have it, the president-elect reached Philadelphia, birth-place of the United States, on George Washington's birthday. Inside Independence Hall, where the Declaration of Independence had been adopt-ed and signed, Lincoln gave an emotional speech. He would rather be assas-sinated here, he said, than surrender Independence Hall to the Confederacy.

I am filled with deep emotion at finding myself standing here in the place where were collected together the wisdom, the patriotism, the devotion to principle, from which sprang the institutions under which we live. You have kindly suggest-ed to me that in my hands is the task of restoring peace to our distracted country. I can say in return . . . that all the political sentiments I entertain have been drawn, so far as I have been able to draw them, from the sentiments which originated, and were given to the world from this hall in which we stand.

Abraham Lincoln raises the American flag outside Independence Hall in Philadelphia on George Washington's birthday in 1861. Notice the spectators in the trees.

I have never had a feeling politically that did not spring from the sentiments embodied in the Declaration of Independence. (Great cheering.) I have often pondered over the dangers which were incurred by the men who assembled here and adopted that Declaration of Independence—I have pondered over the toils that were endured by the officers and soldiers of the army, who achieved that Independence. (Applause.) I have often inquired of myself, what great principle or idea it was that kept this Confederacy so long together. It was not the mere matter of the separation of the colonies from the mother land; but something in that Declaration giving liberty, not alone to the people of this country, but hope to the world for all future time. (Great applause.) It was that which gave promise that in due time the weights should be lifted from the shoulders of all men, and that *all* should have an equal chance. (Cheers.) This is the sentiment embodied in that Declaration of Independence.

<hr />

FROM HIS FIRST INAUGURAL ADDRESS MARCH 4, 1861
Washington

The divided country watched and waited as Lincoln took the oath of office as president. Lincoln's inaugural address was designed to reassure southerners that he meant them no harm. The speech was magnificent, but it did not convince the South.

> Why should there not be a patient confidence in the ultimate justice of the people? Is there any better, or equal hope, in the world? In our present differences, is either party without faith of being in the right? If the Almighty Ruler of nations, with his eternal truth and justice, be on your side of the North, or on yours of the South, that truth, and that justice, will surely prevail, by the judgment of this great tribunal, the American people.

> By the frame of the government under which we live, this same people have wisely given their public servants but little

power for mischief; and have, with equal wisdom, provided for the return of that little to their own hands at very short intervals.

While the people retain their virtue, and vigilence, no administration, by any extreme of wickedness or folly, can very seriously injure the government, in the short space of four years.

My countrymen, one and all, think calmly and *well*, upon this whole subject. Nothing valuable can be lost by taking time. If there be an object to *hurry* any of you, in hot haste, to a step which you would never take *deliberately*, that object will be frustrated by taking time; but no good object can be frustrated by it. Such of you as are now dissatisfied, still have the old Constitution unimpaired, and, on the sensitive point, the

Lincoln's first inauguration, on March 4, 1861.

laws of your own framing under it; while the new administration will have no immediate power, if it would, to change either. If it were admitted that you who are dissatisfied, hold the right side in the dispute, there still is no single good reason for precipitate action. Intelligence, patriotism, Christianity, and a firm reliance on Him, who has never yet forsaken this favored land, are still competent to adjust, in the best way, all our present difficulty.

In *your* hands, my dissatisfied fellow countrymen, and not in *mine*, is the momentous issue of civil war. The government will not assail *you*. You can have no conflict, without being yourselves the aggressors. *You* have no oath registered in Heaven to destroy the government, while *I* shall have the most solemn one to "preserve, protect and defend" it.

I am loth to close. We are not enemies, but friends. We must not be enemies. Though passion may have strained, it must not break our bonds of affection. The mystic chords of memory, stre[t]ching from every battle-field, and patriot grave, to every living heart and hearthstone, all over this broad land, will yet swell the chorus of the Union, when again touched, as surely they will be, by the better angels of our nature.

⟹◆⟸

TO THE PARENTS OF A DEAD HERO-MAY 25, 1861
Letter to Ephraim and Phoebe Ellsworth

Ephraim Elmer Ellsworth was the first Union officer killed in the Civil War. He was shot to death by an angry hotel keeper across the river from Washington in Alexandria, Virginia, on May 24, 1861. Ellsworth had just torn down a Confederate flag that was flying over the hotel. The dead hero was just twenty-four years old. Ellsworth was honored with a White House funeral. Lincoln mourned deeply. The president had known young Ellsworth back in Illinois and had come to admire him greatly. This is the loving tribute that Lincoln wrote to the slain soldier's mother and father.

To the Father and Mother of Col.
Elmer E. Ellsworth:

My dear Sir and Madam, In the untimely loss of your noble son, our affliction here, is scarcely less than your own. So much of promised usefulness to one's country, and of bright hopes for one's self and friends, have rarely been so suddenly dashed, as in his fall. In size, in years, and in youthful appearance, a boy

Ephraim Elmer Ellsworth, the first Union officer killed in the Civil War.

only, his power to command men, was surpassingly great. This power, combined with a fine intellect, an indomitable energy, and a taste altogether military, constituted in him, as seemed to me, the best natural talent, in that department, I ever knew. And yet he was singularly modest and deferential in social intercourse. My acquaintance with him began less than two years ago; yet through the latter half of the intervening period, it was as intimate as the disparity of our ages, and my engrossing engagements, would permit. To me, he appeared to have no indulgences or pastimes; and I never heard him utter a profane, or an intemperate word. What was conclusive of his good heart, he never forgot his parents. The honors he labored for so laudably, and, in the sad end, so gallantly gave his life, he meant for them, no less than for himself.

In the hope that it may be no intrusion upon the sacredness of your sorrow, I have ventured to address you this tribute to

the memory of my young friend, and your brave and early fall-
en child.

May God give you that consolation which is beyond all
earthly power. Sincerely your friend in a common affliction—

A. LINCOLN

⟹◆⟸

FROM AN INDEPENDENCE DAY MESSAGE TO CONGRESS-JULY 4, 1861
Washington

Lincoln had convinced himself that, if necessary, war must be waged to
reunite the country. Now he had to convince Congress. The House and Senate
returned to Washington for a special emergency session in time for
Independence Day. Lincoln used the occasion to send this inspiring message. It
was read aloud to Congress that day, and two weeks later Union and
Confederate armies fought each other for the first time at the Battle of Bull Run.

This is essentially a People's contest. On the side of the
Union, it is a struggle for maintaining in the world, that form,
and substance of government, whose leading object is, to ele-
vate the condition of men—to lift artificial weights from all
shoulders—to clear the paths of laudable pursuit for all—to
afford all, an unfettered start, and a fair chance, in the race of
life. Yielding to partial, and temporary departures, from necessity, this is the leading object of the government for whose existence we contend. . . .

Our popular government has often been called an experi-
ment. Two points in it, our people have already settled—the
successful *establishing*, and the successful *administering* of it. One
still remains—its successful *maintenance* against a formidable
[internal] attempt to overthrow it. It is now for them to demon-
strate to the world, that those who can fairly carry an election,
can also suppress a rebellion—that ballots are the rightful, and

New York's Seventh Regiment marches down Broadway in New York City as it departs for the war.

peaceful, successors of bullets; and that when ballots have fairly, and constitutionally, decided, there can be no successful appeal, back to bullets; that there can be no successful appeal, except to ballots themselves, at succeeding elections. Such will be a great lesson of peace; teaching men that what they cannot take by an election, neither can they take it by a war—teaching all, the folly of being the beginners of a war.

<hr />

A JOB RECOMMENDATION-OCTOBER 17, 1861
Letter to George D. Ramsay

From the moment he moved into the White House, Lincoln was bombarded with requests for government jobs. This was understandable: he was the first Republican ever elected president, and now Republicans wanted the jobs that Democrats had held for so long. The new president saw hundreds of job seekers personally, usually telling them bluntly that he could not help them. But when one woman arrived to say her sons were willing to work hard, Lincoln could not resist. He wrote this letter to the commander of the Washington arsenal.

Majr. Ramsay
My dear Sir

The lady—bearer of this—says she has two sons who want to work. Set them at it, if possible. Wanting to work is so rare a merit, that it should be encouraged. Yours truly

A. LINCOLN

Lincoln in 1861.

Reply to the "Prayer of Twenty Millions"
August 22, 1862
Letter to the New York Tribune

On August 19, 1862, a pro-Union newspaper, the *New York Tribune*, published an editorial criticizing Lincoln's policy on slavery. Denouncing Lincoln for failing to move quickly to free the slaves, editor Horace Greeley called the president "preposterous." Lincoln replied with this famous letter to the editor, defending his determination to fight to save the Union, not necessarily to free the slaves. What Greeley and the readers of the *Tribune* did not know was that at the time Lincoln wrote the letter, he had also written the Emancipation Proclamation. He was merely waiting for the right moment to issue it. The proclamation would be announced within a month, on September 22.

> Hon. Horace Greely:
> Dear Sir
>
> I have just read yours of the 19th. addressed to myself through the New-York Tribune. If there be in it any statements, or assumptions of fact, which I may know to be erroneous, I do not, now and here, controvert them. If there be in it any inferences which I may believe to be falsely drawn, I do not now and here, argue against them. If there be perceptable in it an impatient and dictatorial tone, I waive it in deference to an old friend, whose heart I have always supposed to be right.
> As to the policy I "seem to be pursuing" as you say, I have not meant to leave any one in doubt.
> I would save the Union. I would save it the shortest way under the Constitution. The sooner the national authority can be restored; the nearer the Union will be "the Union as it was." If there be those who would not save the Union, unless they could at the same time *save* slavery, I do not agree with them. If there be those who would not save the Union unless they could at the same time *destroy* slavery, I do not agree with them. My paramount object in this struggle *is* to save the Union, and is *not* either to save or to destroy slavery. If I could

save the Union without freeing *any* slave I would do it, and if I could save it by freeing *all* the slaves I would do it; and if I could save it by freeing some and leaving others alone I would also do that. What I do about slavery, and the colored race, I do because I believe it helps to save the Union; and what I forbear, I forbear because I do *not* believe it would help to save the Union. I shall do *less* whenever I shall believe what I am doing hurts the cause, and I shall do *more* whenever I shall believe doing more will help the cause. I shall try to correct errors when shown to be errors; and I shall adopt new views so fast as they shall appear to be true views.

I have here stated my purpose according to my view of *official* duty; and I intend no modification of my oft-expressed *personal* wish that all men every where could be free. Yours,

A. LINCOLN

Horace Greeley.

This view of Lincoln in front of the Capitol is ironic. The sixteenth president did not have a particularly good relationship with Congress.

FROM HIS FIRST ANNUAL MESSAGE TO CONGRESS
DECEMBER 1, 1862
Washington

Lincoln's best-known State of the Union address, then called the Annual Message to Congress, included proposals that slavery be abolished in loyal slave states such as Maryland and Delaware by the year 1900. But the message is best remembered for its magnificent final paragraph.

> Fellow-citizens, *we* cannot escape history. We of this Congress and this administration, will be remembered in spite of ourselves. No personal significance, or insignificance, can spare one or another of us. The fiery trial through which we pass, will light us down, in honor or dishonor, to the latest generation.

We *say* we are for the Union. The world will not forget that we say this. We know how to save the Union. The world knows we do know how to save it. We—even *we here*—hold the power, and bear the responsibility. In *giving* freedom to the *slave*, we *assure* freedom to the *free*—honorable alike in what we give, and what we preserve. We shall nobly save, or meanly lose, the last best, hope of earth. Other means may succeed; this could not fail. The way is plain, peaceful, generous, just—a way which, if followed, the world will forever applaud, and God must forever bless.

—————♦—————

SYMPATHY FOR A DEAD HERO-DECEMBER 23, 1862
Letter to Fanny McCullough

Lincoln wrote this magnificent letter when he learned of the death of cavalry officer William McCullough in Mississippi. Lincoln had known him back in Illinois. Now he heard that McCullough's daughter, Fanny, was so overcome with grief that her family worried that she would go insane. Lincoln hoped that his eloquent note would help her regain her health.

Dear Fanny

It is with deep grief that I learn of the death of your kind and brave Father; and, especially, that it is affecting your young heart beyond what is common in such cases. In this sad world of ours, sorrow comes to all; and, to the young, it comes with bitterest agony, because it takes them unawares. The older have learned to ever expect it. I am anxious to afford some alleviation of your present distress. Perfect relief is not possible, except with time. You can not now realize that you will ever feel better. Is not this so? And yet it is a mistake. You are sure to be happy again. To know this, which is certainly true, will make you some less miserable now. I have had experience enough to know what I say; and you need only to believe it, to feel better at once. The memory of your dear Father, instead of an agony,

will yet be a sad sweet feeling in your heart, of a purer, and holi-
er sort than you have known before.

Please present my kind regards to your afflicted mother.

Your sincere friend
A. LINCOLN

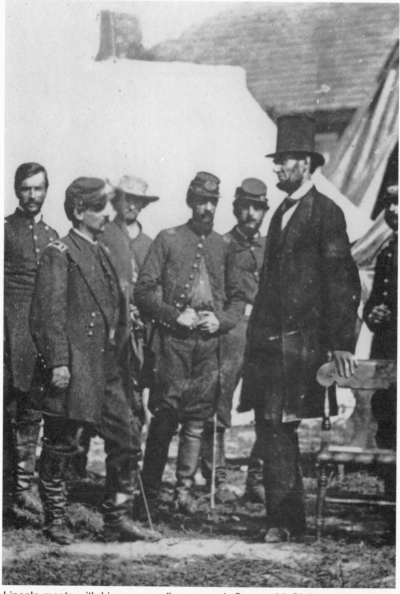

Lincoln meets with his commanding general, George McClellan, at Antietam,
Maryland, in October 1862, two weeks after the Union won a major battle there.

THE FINAL EMANCIPATION PROCLAMATION
JANUARY 1, 1863

Time ran out for slavery on New Year's Day, 1863. Just as he had promised on September 22, 1862, Lincoln issued a final Emancipation Proclamation declaring slaves in the Confederate states free and vowing to use the Union military to maintain their freedom. The document was written in legal language. It was not inspiring, but its effect on America was greater than that of any words written by any leader since the Revolutionary War. Lincoln knew he would be remembered for all time for this act. When his hand trembled as he prepared to sign it, he put down the pen and paused. He did not want people to look at the document years later, see his shaky handwriting, and conclude that he was uncertain about his decision.

By the President of the United States of America:
A Proclamation.

Whereas, on the twentysecond day of September, in the year of our Lord one thousand eight hundred and sixty two, a proclamation was issued by the President of the United States, containing, among other things, the following, towit:

"That on the first day of January, in the year of our Lord one thousand eight hundred and sixty-three, all persons held as slaves within any State or designated part of a State, the people whereof shall then be in rebellion against the United States, shall be then, thenceforward, and forever free; and the Executive Government of the United States, including the military and naval authority thereof, will recognize and maintain the freedom of such persons, and will do no act or acts to repress such persons, or any of them, in any efforts they may make for their actual freedom.

"That the Executive will, on the first day of January aforesaid, by proclamation, designate the States and parts of States, if any, in which the people thereof, respectively, shall then be in rebellion against the United States; and the fact that any State, or the people thereof, shall on that day be, in good faith, represented in the Congress of the United States by members

Abraham Lincoln and His Emancipation Proclamation.

chosen thereto at elections wherein a majority of the qualified voters of such State shall have participated, shall, in the absence of strong countervailing testimony, be deemed conclusive evidence that such State, and the people thereof, are not then in rebellion against the United States."

Now, therefore I, Abraham Lincoln, President of the United States, by virtue of the power in me vested as Commander-in-Chief, of the Army and Navy of the United States in time of actual armed rebellion against authority and government of the United States, and as a fit and necessary war measure for suppressing said rebellion, do, on this first day of January, in the year of our Lord one thousand eight hundred and sixty three, and in accordance with my purpose so to do publicly proclaimed for the full period of one hundred days, from the day first above mentioned, order and designate as the States and parts of States wherein the people thereof respectively, are this day in rebellion against the United States, the following, towit:

Arkansas, Texas, Louisiana, (except the Parishes of St. Bernard, Plaquemines, Jefferson, St. Johns, St. Charles, St. James[,] Ascension, Assumption, Terrebonne, Lafourche, St. Mary, St. Martin, and Orleans, including the City of New-Orleans) Mississippi, Alabama, Florida, Georgia, South-Carolina, North-Carolina, and Virginia (except the fortyeight counties designated as West Virginia, and also the counties of Berkley, Accomac, Northampton, Elizabeth-City, York, Princess Ann, and Norfolk, including the cities of Norfolk & Portsmouth[)]; and which excepted parts are, for the present, left precisely as if this proclamation were not issued.

And by virtue of the power, and for the purpose aforesaid, I do order and declare that all persons held as slaves within said designated States, and parts of States, are, and henceforward shall be free; and that the Executive government of the United States, including the military and naval authorities thereof, will recognize and maintain the freedom of said persons.

And I hereby enjoin upon the people so declared to be free to abstain from all violence, unless in necessary self-defence; and I recommend to them that, in all cases when allowed, they labor faithfully for reasonable wages.

Francis B. Carpenter's famous painting of Lincoln reading the Emancipation Proclamation for the first time to his cabinet on July 22, 1862.

And I further declare and make known, that such persons of suitable condition, will be received into the armed service of the United States to garrison forts, positions, stations, and other places, and to man vessels of all sorts in said service.

And upon this act, sincerely believed to be an act of justice, warranted by the Constitution, upon military necessity, I invoke the considerate judgment of mankind, and the gracious favor of Almighty God.

In witness whereof, I have hereunto set my hand and caused the seal of the United States to be affixed.

Done at the City of Washington, this first day of January, in the year of our Lord one thousand eight hundred and sixty three, and of the Independence of the United States of America the eighty-seventh.

By the President:
ABRAHAM LINCOLN

A NIGHTMARE ABOUT HIS SON—JUNE 9, 1863
Telegram to Mary Lincoln

Lincoln often had disturbing dreams, and he usually told others whenever he did. His wife and son were visiting Philadelphia when he had one particularly upsetting nightmare. This is the urgent message he wrote to Mary in response. It shows that he took his dreams quite seriously.

Lincoln often arranged for Tad to receive miniature uniforms and weapons. Obviously he worried about these gifts, too.

> Mrs. Lincoln
> Philadelphia, Pa.
>
> Think you better put "Tad's" pistol away. I had an ugly dream about him.
>
> A. LINCOLN

Mathew Brady's photograph of Lincoln's son Tad.

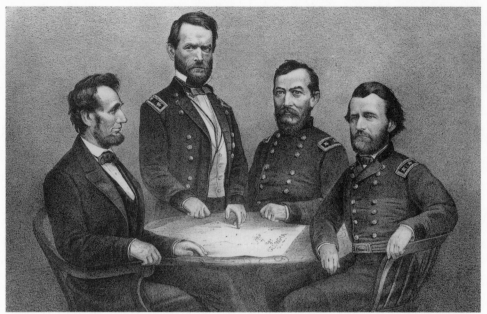

President Lincoln at Genl. Grant's Headquarters. From left to right: Lincoln, William T. Sherman, Philip H. Sheridan, and Ulysses S. Grant.

CONGRATULATING A VICTORIOUS GENERAL
JULY 13, 1863
Letter to Ulysses S. Grant

The city of Vicksburg, Mississippi, surrendered to General Grant on July 4, 1863. Lincoln sent this letter of congratulations a few days later. It is difficult to imagine a modern president admitting he was wrong. Lincoln does so here.

My dear General

I do not remember that you and I ever met personally. I write this now as a grateful acknowledgment for the almost inestimable service you have done the country. I wish to say a word further. When you first reached the vicinity of Vicksburg, I thought you should do, what you finally did—march the troops across the neck, run the batteries with the transports, and thus go below; and I never had any faith, except a general hope that you knew better than I, that the Yazoo Pass expedition, and the like, could succeed. When you got below, and took Port-Gibson, Grand Gulf, and vicinity, I thought you should go down the river and join Gen. Banks; and when you turned Northward East of the Big Black, I feared it was a mistake. I now wish to make the personal acknowledgment that you were right, and I was wrong.

Yours very truly
A. LINCOLN

BEGGING HIS COLLEGE STUDENT SON TO WRITE HOME-JULY 14, 1863
Letter to Robert T. Lincoln

Like all parents, Lincoln expected his son Robert, a college student, to write home more often. This telegram was sent by the worried father when Robert was heading to Washington for a family visit.

Robt. T. Lincoln
New-York. 5th. Av. Hotel —

Why do I hear no more of you?

A. LINCOLN

Robert Lincoln.

Tad Lincoln in his soldier's uniform around 1861. Note the facial hair, probably added by himself.

BAD NEWS FOR TAD: HIS PET GOAT VANISHES
AUGUST 8, 1863
From a Letter to Mary Lincoln

Young Tad Lincoln's pets, particularly his goats, were the terrors of the White House. One of his goats, Nanny, raced through the East Room and sometimes ate the furniture. But Tad so loved his animals that his father allowed him to keep them. In the summer of 1863, Mary Lincoln took Tad on vacation to the Vermont mountains, leaving no one to look after the goat. Nanny soon vanished, and Lincoln was forced to report her loss to Mary. One can almost imagine poor Tad's reaction when he heard the bad news.

My dear Wife. All as well as usual, and no particular trouble any way. I put the money into the Treasury at five per cent, with the previlege of withdrawing it any time upon thirty days' notice. I suppose you are glad to learn this. Tell dear Tad, poor

"Nanny Goat," is lost; and Mrs. Cuthbert & I are in distress about it. The day you left Nanny was found resting herself, and chewing her little cud, on the middle of Tad's bed. But now she's gone! The gardener kept complaining that she destroyed the flowers, till it was concluded to bring her down to the White House. This was done, and the second day she had disappeared, and has not been heard of since. This is the last we know of poor "Nanny[.]". . .

Affectionately
A. LINCOLN

HUSBAND MISSES WIFE-SEPTEMBER 21, 1863
Telegram to Mary Lincoln

Lincoln missed Mary whenever she traveled, but especially when she headed north in the summer months to escape the heat in Washington. Eager that she cut short one such vacation, Lincoln wrote this rather romantic plea for her return.

First Lady Mary Lincoln in 1861.

Mrs. A Lincoln
Fifth Avenue Hotel New-York

The air is so clear and cool, and apparantly healthy, that I would be glad for you to come. Nothing very particular, but I would be glad [to] see you and Tad.

A Lincoln

⟹◆⟸

THE GETTYSBURG ADDRESS - NOVEMBER 19, 1863
Gettysburg, Pennsylvania

When the Battle of Gettysburg ended in July, the little Pennsylvania town where it was fought was littered with the bodies of dead soldiers. Village leaders decided to build a national cemetery and bury the battle dead together. Then they organized a solemn ceremony to dedicate the cemetery and invited Lincoln to attend and give "a few appropriate remarks." The president was not asked to deliver the major speech of the day. That honor was given to the famous orator Edward Everett, who responded with a poetic, two-hour-long performance. It was just the kind of formal, classical oration expected on such an occasion. Lincoln's speech was not. The president spoke for only two minutes at Gettysburg, but it was one of the most beautiful speeches ever delivered. Not only did it offer an eloquent tribute to the heroes who had died so that "the nation might live," but it also told America that it must now be dedicated to "a new birth of freedom" that would guarantee equality and justice for all. Such a dream, Lincoln insisted, was well worth fighting for—even dying for. If it is true that Lincoln's Emancipation Proclamation was not written in an inspiring way, he made up for it at Gettysburg. It might even be said that if the Emancipation Proclamation was the "prose" of liberty—legally important but not beautiful—the Gettysburg Address was the "poetry." The legend persists that the address was not appreciated at the time, but this is not true. Many newspapers of the day praised the president lavishly, and Edward Everett wrote to Lincoln, "I should be glad, if . . . I came as near to the central idea of the occasion in two hours as you did in two minutes."

Crowds gather at the dedication of Gettysburg National Cemetery, in Gettysburg, Pennsylvania, on November 19, 1863.

Four score and seven years ago our fathers brought forth on this continent, a new nation, conceived in Liberty, and dedicated to the proposition that all men are created equal.

Now we are engaged in a great civil war; testing whether that nation, or any nation so conceived and so dedicated, can long endure. We are met on a great battle-field of that war. We have come to dedicate a portion of that field, as a final resting place for those who here gave their lives that that nation might live. It is altogether fitting and proper that we should do this.

But, in a larger sense, we can not dedicate—we can not consecrate—we can not hallow—this ground. The brave men, living and dead, who struggled here have consecrated it, far above our poor power to add or detract. The world will little note, nor long remember what we say here, but it can never forget what they did here. It is for us the living, rather, to be dedicated here to the unfinished work which they who fought here have thus far so nobly advanced. It is rather for us to be here dedicated to the great task remaining before us—that from these honored dead we take increased devotion to that cause for which they gave the last full measure of devotion—that we here highly resolve that these dead shall not have died in vain—that this nation, under God, shall have a new birth of freedom—and that government of the people, by the people, for the people, shall not perish from the earth.

Lincoln in 1864.

URGING THAT BLACKS BE ALLOWED TO VOTE
MARCH 13, 1864
Letter to Governor Michael Hahn

After Union armies conquered Louisiana, the onetime slave state was reorganized as a free state. Lincoln took the opportunity to urge its new governor, Michael Hahn, to allow African Americans to vote. Even though Lincoln was asking for voting rights only for war veterans or the educated, it was a giant step forward for him—and eventually, for the country. It was the first time Lincoln had recommended the vote for black people. The state rejected the president's recommendation.

Private
Hon. Michael Hahn
My dear Sir:

I congratulate you on having fixed your name in history as the first-free-state Governor of Louisiana. Now you are about to have a Convention which, among other things, will probably define the elective franchise. I barely suggest for your private consideration, whether some of the colored people may not be let in—as, for instance, the very intelligent, and especially those who have fought gallantly in our ranks. They would probably help, in some trying time to come, to keep the jewel of liberty within the family of freedom. But this is only a suggestion, not to the public, but to you alone. Yours truly

A. LINCOLN

———◆———

A THOUGHT ON THE EVILS OF SLAVERY
MARCH 22, 1864

When Lincoln was asked for an autograph that could be sold to raise money for soldiers' charities, he responded with this thought about slavery.

I never knew a man who wished to be himself a slave. Consider if you know any *good* thing, that no man desires for himself.

A. LINCOLN

———◆———

RESPONDING TO CHILDREN'S PLEA FOR FREEDOM
APRIL 5, 1864
Letter to Mrs. Horace Mann

In the spring of 1864, a group of 195 children from Concord, Massachusetts, signed and sent to Lincoln a petition asking that all slave children everywhere be freed. The Massachusetts young people also donated one cent each or more to help slave children. As these generous youngsters knew, the Emancipation Proclamation had freed slaves only in the Confederate states. Slavery was still legal in the southern states that remained in the Union. Lincoln wrote the following reply to what he called the "Little People's Petition." It was sent to Mrs. Horace Mann, the Concord woman who had organized the petition drive. The president claimed he had no power to free slaves in the loyal states, but at the time he was working to build support for an amendment to the Constitution that would end slavery everywhere. The Thirteenth Amendment became law a few months after Lincoln died.

> Mrs. Horace Mann,
> Madam,
>
> The petition of persons under eighteen, praying that I would free all slave children, and the heading of which petition it appears you wrote, was handed me a few days since by Senator Sumner. Please tell these little people I am very glad their young hearts are so full of just and generous sympathy, and that, while I have not the power to grant all they ask, I trust they will remember that God has, and that, as it seems, He wills to do it. Yours truly
>
> A. LINCOLN

<hr />

"A GOOD DEFINITION" OF LIBERTY
APRIL 18, 1864
From an Address at a Sanitary Fair, Baltimore, Maryland

Lincoln traveled to Baltimore to visit a huge sanitary, or charity, fair. Asked for a speech, he responded with these brief remarks, using the occasion to remind listeners that the war had helped America to understand the value of liberty. As he often did, Lincoln used comparisons to farm animals to make his point—that race and color do not matter when it comes to the right to freedom.

The world has never had a good definition of the word liberty, and the American people, just now, are much in want of one. We all declare for liberty; but in using the same *word* we do not all mean the same *thing*. With some the word liberty may mean for each man to do as he pleases with himself, and the product of his labor; while with others the same word may mean for some men to do as they please with other men, and the product of other men's labor. Here are two, not only different, but incompatable things, called by the same name—liberty. And it follows that each of the things is, by the respective parties, called by two different and incompatable names—liberty and tyranny.

The shepherd drives the wolf from the sheep's throat, for which the sheep thanks the shepherd as a *liberator*, while the wolf denounces him for the same act as the destroyer of liberty, especially as the sheep was a black one. Plainly the sheep and the wolf are not agreed upon a definition of the word liberty; and precisely the same difference prevails to-day among us human creatures, even in the North, and all professing to love liberty. Hence we behold the processes by which thousands are daily passing from under the yoke of bondage, hailed by some as the advance of liberty, and bewailed by others as the destruction of all liberty. Recently, as it seems, the people of Maryland have been doing something to define liberty; and thanks to them that, in what they have done, the wolf's dictionary, has been repudiated.

Father and Goats Are Fine-April 28, 1864

Telegram to Mary Lincoln

Lincoln's wife and young son Tad were traveling in New York when the president received the following telegram from Mary: "Please send me by mail to-day a check for $50 directed to me, . . . Tad says are the goats well." Lincoln sent the following reply.

Mrs. A. Lincoln
Metropolitan Hotel
New-York.

The draft will go to you. Tell Tad the goats and father are very well—especially the goats.

A. LINCOLN.

Abraham and Tad Lincoln.

———◅◆▻———

SPEECH TO AN OHIO REGIMENT-AUGUST 22, 1864
The White House

Lincoln made this touching speech to a regiment of Ohio soldiers returning home after months of service in the Union army.

I suppose you are going home to see your families and friends. For the service you have done in this great struggle in which we are engaged I present you sincere thanks for myself and the country. I almost always feel inclined, when I happen to say anything to soldiers, to impress upon them in a few brief remarks the importance of success in this contest. It is not merely for to-day, but for all time to come that we should perpetuate for our children's children this great and free government, which we have enjoyed all our lives. I beg you to remember this, not merely for my sake, but for yours. I happen temporarily to occupy this big White House. I am a living witness that any one of your children may look to come here as my father's child has. It is in order that each of you may have through this free government which we have enjoyed, an open field and a fair chance for your industry, enterprise and intelligence; that you may all have equal privileges in the race of life, with all its desirable human aspirations. It is for this the struggle should be maintained, that we may not lose our birthright—not only for one, but for two or three years. The nation is worth fighting for, to secure such an inestimable jewel.

Lincoln on February 9, 1864.

A campaign banner for the Republican ticket in the 1864 presidential election. The vice-presidential candidate was Andrew Johnson of Tennessee. Lincoln and Johnson won the election in November.

THE "BIXBY LETTER"-NOVEMBER 21, 1864
Letter to Lydia Bixby

The governor of Massachusetts asked Lincoln to write this sympathy letter to Lydia Bixby, whose five sons had died in the war. Later it was learned that only two Bixby boys had been killed in battle. At least one had deserted, another was either a prisoner of war or had been honorably discharged, and yet another had left the army very much alive. But the letter was so beautifully written it has been remembered. The original handwritten copy has never been found.

Dear Madam,—I have been shown in the files of the War Department a statement of the Adjutant General of Massachusetts, that you are the mother of five sons who have died gloriously on the field of battle.

I feel how weak and fruitless must be any words of mine which should attempt to beguile you from the grief of a loss so overwhelming. But I cannot refrain from tendering to you the consolation that may be found in the thanks of the Republic they died to save.

I pray that our Heavenly Father may assuage the anguish of

your bereavement, and leave you only the cherished memory of the loved and lost, and the solemn pride that must be yours, to have laid so costly a sacrifice upon the altar of Freedom. Yours, very sincerely and respectfully,

A. LINCOLN.

A photographer captured Lincoln as he delivers his second inaugural address.

HIS SECOND INAUGURAL ADDRESS-MARCH 4, 1865
Washington

Clouds filled the sky when Lincoln rose to deliver his second inaugural address outside the Capitol. But as he began speaking, the sun suddenly burst through, and the crowd gasped. Lincoln's speech that day was one of the shortest—and finest—inaugural addresses ever given. He began by blaming the sin of slavery for the terrible bloodshed of the Civil War. He ended by pleading for a lasting peace. Four weeks later, Robert E. Lee surrendered to Ulysses S. Grant, and Lincoln's wish was granted: the war was over. Some experts believe that this was Lincoln's best speech, even greater than the Gettysburg Address. Note how he used an unusual word—*appearing* instead of *appearance*—to get the attention of his audience.

Fellow Countrymen:

At this second appearing to take the oath of the presidential office, there is less occasion for an extended address than there was at the first. Then a statement, somewhat in detail, of a course to be pursued, seemed fitting and proper. Now, at the expiration of four years, during which public declarations have been constantly called forth on every point and phase of the great contest which still absorbs the attention, and engrosses the enerergies [sic] of the nation, little that is new could be presented. The progress of our arms, upon which all else chiefly depends, is as well known to the public as to myself; and it is, I trust, reasonably satisfactory and encouraging to all. With high hope for the future, no prediction in regard to it is ventured.

On the occasion corresponding to this four years ago, all thoughts were anxiously directed to an impending civil-war. All dreaded it—all sought to avert it. While the inaugeral address was being delivered from this place, devoted altogether to *saving* the Union without war, insurgent agents were in the city seeking to *destroy* it without war—seeking to dissol[v]e the Union, and divide effects, by negotiation. Both parties deprecated war; but one of them would *make* war rather than let the nation survive; and the other would *accept* war rather than let it perish. And the war came.

One eighth of the whole population were colored slaves, not distributed generally over the Union, but localized in the Southern part of it. These slaves constituted a peculiar and powerful interest. All knew that this interest was, somehow, the cause of the war. To strengthen, perpetuate, and extend this interest was the object for which the insurgents would rend the Union, even by war; while the government claimed no right to do more than to restrict the territorial enlargement of it. Neither party expected for the war, the magnitude, or the duration, which it has already attained. Neither anticipated that the *cause* of the conflict might cease with, or even before, the conflict itself should cease. Each looked for an easier triumph, and a result less fundamental and astounding. Both read the same Bible, and pray to the same God; and each invokes His aid against the other. It may seem strange that any men should dare to ask a just God's assistance in wringing their bread from the sweat of other men's faces; but let us judge not that we be not judged. The prayers of both could not be answered; that of neither has been answered fully. The Almighty has His own purposes. "Woe unto the world because of offences! for it must needs be that offences come; but woe to that man by whom the offence cometh!" If we shall suppose that American Slavery is one of those offences which, in the providence of God, must needs come, but which, having continued through His appointed time, He now wills to remove, and that He gives to both North and South, this terrible war, as the woe due to those by whom the offence came, shall we discern therein any departure from those divine attributes which the believers in a Living God always ascribe to Him? Fondly do we hope—fervently do we pray—that this mighty scourge of war may speedily pass away. Yet, if God wills that it continue, until all the wealth piled by the bond-man's two hundred and fifty years of unrequited toil shall be sunk, and until every drop of blood drawn with the lash, shall be paid by another drawn with the sword, as was said three thousand years ago, so still it must be said "the judgments of the Lord, are true and righteous altogether."

With malice toward none; with charity for all; with firmness in the right, as God gives us to see the right, let us strive on to finish the work we are in; to bind up the nation's wounds; to care for him who shall have borne the battle, and for his widow, and his orphan—to do all which may achieve and cherish a just, and a lasting peace, among ourselves, and with all nations.

Lincoln sat for photographer Alexander Gardner a few days before his fifty-sixth birthday in 1865.

A LIFELONG BELIEF IN FREEDOM—MARCH 17, 1865
Speech to Indiana Soldiers, Washington

Lincoln made these brief but powerful remarks to a regiment of Indiana soldiers who had fought bravely for the Union in North Carolina. Less than a month later, the war was over at last, and many of the soldiers he had met that day had gone home. Then on April 14, Abraham Lincoln was shot by John Wilkes Booth. The president died the following day.

FELLOW CITIZENS. A few words only. I was born in Kentucky, raised in Indiana, reside in Illinois, and now here, it is my duty to care equally for the good people of all the States. I am to-day glad of seeing it in the power of an Indianana regiment to present this captured flag to the good governor of their State. And yet I would not wish to compliment Indiana above other states, remembering that all have done so well. There are but few aspects of this great war on which I have not already expressed my views by speaking or writing. There is one—the recent effort of our erring bretheren, sometimes so-called, to employ the slaves in their armies. The great question with them has been; "will the negro fight for them?" They ought to know better than we; and, doubtless, do know better than we. I may incidentally remark, however, that having, in my life, heard many arguments,—or strings of words meant to pass for arguments,—intended to show that the negro ought to be a slave, that if he shall now really fight to keep himself a slave, it will be a far better argument why [he] should remain a slave than I have ever before heard. He, perhaps, ought to be a slave, if he desires it ardently enough to fight for it. Or, if one out of four will, for his own freedom, fight to keep the other three in slavery, he ought to be a slave for his selfish meanness. I have always thought that all men should be free; but if any should be slaves it should be first those who desire it for *themselves*, and secondly those who *desire* it for *others*. Whenever [I] hear any one, arguing for slavery I feel a strong impulse to see it tried on him personally.

There is one thing about the negroes fighting for the rebels which we can know as well [as] they can; and that is that they can not, at [the] same time fight in their armies, and stay at home and make bread for them. And this being known and remembered we can have but little concern whether they become soldiers or not. I am rather in favor of the measure; and would at any time if I could, have loaned them a vote to carry it. We have to reach the bottom of the insurgent resources; and that they employ, or seriously think of employing, the slaves as soldiers, gives us glimpses of the bottom. Therefore I am glad of what we learn on this subject.

⧩◆⧨

ABRAHAM LINCOLN
➤ His Life Story, Year by Year ➤

1809

Abraham Lincoln is born on February 12 in a one-room, dirt-floor log cabin near the town of Hodgenville in central Kentucky. His parents, Thomas and Nancy, can barely read and write.

1811

His family moves to a new farm near Knob Creek, Kentucky. Young Abraham will learn how to plant seeds and pick crops.

1815

Abraham goes to school for the first time. It is a so-called "blab school"—all students say their lessons out loud.

1816

The family moves to Indiana and builds a new log cabin on Little Pigeon Creek.

1818

Abraham's mother dies after drinking poisoned milk. Abe nearly dies, too—after being kicked in the head by a horse—but he recovers.

1819

Abraham's father marries Sarah Bush Johnston, who becomes a loving stepmother to Abraham. She encourages him to read, write, and study. His father prefers that he work.

1820

Abraham goes back to school and begins reading books. He studies the Bible, borrows a life story of George Washington, and reads his first novel.

1824

Abraham attends school again. He also must labor on the family farm and becomes particularly skillful at chopping wood and splitting logs into rails to build fences.

1828

Abraham helps pilot a flatboat down the Mississippi River to New Orleans. There he probably sees a slave auction for the first time.

1830

Lincoln, now twenty-one, helps his family move to new land in Illinois. He works with his father to build yet another log cabin.

1831

Lincoln makes his second flatboat trip to New Orleans. Then he leaves his family and settles on his own in the village of New Salem, Illinois. There he wins a legendary wrestling match with local bully Jack Armstrong. He becomes popular with his neighbors. He reads Shakespeare and the Scottish poet Robert Burns. He votes in an election for the first time.

1832

Lincoln runs for his first office, in the Illinois House of Representatives, and loses. In the spring, he serves in the Black Hawk Indian War and is elected captain of his company. He sees no action.

1833

Lincoln becomes postmaster of New Salem and then becomes a surveyor to earn extra money. He is a partner in a local grocery store, but the business fails. When his money runs out, he works as a laborer. This is one of Lincoln's most disappointing years.

1834

Lincoln wins a seat in the Illinois House of Representatives and begins to study law.

1835

His New Salem sweetheart, Ann Rutledge, dies at age twenty-two.

1836

Lincoln is reelected to the Illinois legislature and gets his law license.

1837

Lincoln moves to Springfield to start his life over. He has worked to make the town the new state capital. He ends a brief, halfhearted engagement to Mary Owens and becomes the junior law partner of John T. Stuart.

1838

He is elected to another term in the Illinois House, but he admits he is as lonely in Springfield as he has ever been anywhere.

1839

Lincoln meets his future wife, Mary Todd, a Kentucky woman who has moved to Springfield to live with her sister.

1840

He is reelected to the state legislature and becomes engaged to Mary.

1841

He breaks his engagement to Mary and leaves Stuart's law firm to join a new law partner, Stephen T. Logan.

1842

He begins to see Mary again and marries her on November 4. They move to the Globe Tavern in Springfield.

1843

Abraham loses his party's nomination for Congress, but the Lincolns welcome their first son, Robert.

1844

Abraham and Mary buy a house in Springfield for $1,500. It is the only home Lincoln will ever own. He ends his partnership with Logan and starts his own law practice. His new junior partner is William H. Herndon.

1846

Abraham and Mary's second son, Edward ("Eddie"), is born. Lincoln is elected to Congress as a member of the Whig Party.

1847

He goes to Washington and takes his seat in Congress on December 4. There he speaks out against the Mexican War.

1848

He continues to oppose the Mexican War, alienating some voters back home. His party does not renominate him for Congress.

1849

Finishing his one and only term as a congressman, Lincoln cosponsors an unsuccessful bill to end slavery in new national territories and in Washington, D.C. He returns home to practice law and applies for a patent for an invention to lift boats over shallow water. He tries to get the new president, Zachary Taylor, to appoint him to an important government job, but he fails.

1850

Eddie Lincoln dies. Abraham works hard at the law, spending six months of the year traveling in search of business. Another son, Willie, is born in December.

1851

Lincoln refuses to visit his dying father. He continues to build his law practice.

1852

He supports Whig presidential nominee Winfield Scott but spends much of the year on legal business.

1853

The Lincolns' youngest son, Thomas ("Tad"), is born. Abraham's law practice grows.

1854

When Congress passes a new law expanding slavery, an outraged Lincoln returns to politics. He is elected to the state legislature but declines to serve so that he can run for the U.S. Senate.

1855

He loses the contest for the Senate and continues to practice both law and politics.

1856

Lincoln helps create the new Republican Party in Illinois. He makes fifty speeches for the party's presidential candidate, John C. Frémont, and also enjoys his best year as a lawyer, earning $5,000 for a single case. His fame grows.

1857

He speaks out often against the Supreme Court's Dred Scott decision, which rules that African Americans cannot be citizens. He and Mary make their only trip outside the United States—to Niagara Falls, Canada.

1858

Lincoln is nominated by Illinois Republicans to run against Democrat Stephen A. Douglas for the U.S. Senate. After giving his famous "House Divided" speech in Springfield, he challenges Senator Douglas to a series of debates. The seven Lincoln-Douglas debates become the most famous political confrontation in American history. Lincoln becomes known throughout the country for opposing slavery, but he loses the election.

1859

Beginning to think about running for president, Lincoln gives speeches in several states. He argues passionately against extending slavery to new territories. He writes the story of his life for a newspaper.

1860

In February, he delivers a well-received speech at Cooper Union, a college in New York. It is his first major political appearance in the East. When the Republican Party meets to nominate a candidate for president in May, Lincoln is the surprise winner on the third ballot. He does not campaign for the White House, choosing to stay home and say nothing. That November, he wins only 40 percent of the popular vote. Because his three opponents split the rest of the vote, Lincoln wins the presidency. Some southern states immediately secede from the Union. Lincoln begins to grow a beard after an eleven-year-old girl suggests that his face looks too thin.

1861

Lincoln travels to Washington and is inaugurated the sixteenth president of the United States on March 4. He describes the White House as the biggest and best house he has ever lived in, but Mary insists that it is run-down and begins to redecorate. Meanwhile, more southern states secede. When South Carolina troops attack Fort Sumter in Charleston harbor, the Civil War begins. Lincoln pledges to fight a "People's contest" to save the Union, but his army loses the first battle of the war, at Bull Run, Virginia, in July. Lincoln orders a blockade of southern ports and prepares for a long, bloody war.

1862

In February, Willie Lincoln dies in the White House, and his parents mourn deeply. The Union army wins the Battle of Shiloh in Tennessee but fails to capture the Confederate capital of Richmond, Virginia. Victory comes at Antietam, Maryland, in September. Lincoln immediately issues the Preliminary Emancipation Proclamation. It warns the Confederate states to end their rebellion by January 1 or lose their slaves forever. Lincoln's support in the North diminishes. His party does poorly in the fall congressional elections. Then the Union suffers a terrible loss at the Battle of Fredericksburg in December.

1863

Lincoln signs the final Emancipation Proclamation on January 1. It declares all slaves in rebelling states "thenceforward, and forever free." Now the Union soldiers must fight to make the promise come true. African Americans begin joining the army to fight for their own freedom. The Union loses a battle at Chancellorsville, Virginia, in May. But Lincoln's soldiers capture Vicksburg, Mississippi, and win the Battle of Gettysburg in July. The tide has turned. Lincoln goes to Gettysburg in November to give his most famous speech, the Gettysburg Address.

1864

Lincoln decides to run for reelection even though no president since Andrew Jackson has won a second term. He names Ulysses S. Grant as his general in chief, and the Union army pounds away at the Confederates from west to east. His popularity declines in midyear but soars when the Union captures Atlanta in September. In November, Lincoln defeats Democrat George B. McClellan, receiving 55 percent of the vote (no Confederate state participates).

1865

Congress passes a constitutional amendment ending slavery everywhere. At his second inauguration on March 4, a weary Lincoln asks for "malice toward none" and "charity for all." His army captures Richmond. Lincoln visits there and is cheered by grateful former slaves. On April 9, Robert E. Lee's Confederate army surrenders to Grant, ending the war. On April 11, Lincoln suggests to the public for the first time that free African Americans be allowed to vote. On April 14, a pro-Confederate, deeply racist actor named John Wilkes Booth shoots the president in the back of the head as Lincoln watches a play at Ford's Theatre in Washington. He is carried across the street and dies the following morning. "Now," a witness at his deathbed declares, "he belongs to the ages."

TEXT AND PICTURE CREDITS

Text

The writings of Abraham Lincoln are from Roy P. Basler, ed., Marion Dolores Pratt and Lloyd A. Dunlap, asst. eds., *The Collected Works of Abraham Lincoln,* 8 vols. (New Brunswick, N.J.: Rutgers University Press, 1953), permission courtesy of the Abraham Lincoln Association, Springfield, Illinois.

Picture

The Abraham Lincoln Museum, Cumberland Gap Parkway, Box 2006, Harrogate, Tennessee: 33 (right), 35, 85

From *Harper's Pictorial History of the Civil War* by Alfred H. Guernsey and Henry M. Alden, originally published in 1866: 58, 60, 61

Harriet Beecher Stowe Center, Hartford, CT: 63

Courtesy of the Illinois State Historical Library: 20, 22, 25, 33 (left), 37, 39, 53

Courtesy of the Library of Congress: background cover, 3, 10, 15, 18, 19, 26, 28, 30, 36, 38, 45, 46, 50, 51, 52, 54, 56, 64, 66, 68, 70, 71, 72, 77, 78, 84, 88

Courtesy of The Lincoln Museum, Fort Wayne, Indiana: 12 (#3481), 16 (#2051), 32 (#3481), 73 (#3769), 74 (#4051), 83 (#0-89)

Meg Holzer: 105

University of Michigan Museum of Art, Bequest of Henry C. Lewis, 1895.90: 9, 24

Still Picture Branch of the National Archives and Records Administration: 47 (111-B-4047), 75 (111-B-5864), 82 (111-B-2088)

INDEX

HAROLD HOLZER, vice president for communications at The Metropolitan Museum of Art, is one of the country's leading authorities on the political culture of the Civil War era.

Holzer has authored, coauthored, or edited fourteen books: *The Lincoln Image* (1984), *Changing the Lincoln Image* (1985), and *The Confederate Image* (1987), all with Mark E. Neely, Jr., and Gabor S. Boritt; *The Lincoln Family Album* (1990) and *Mine Eyes Have Seen the Glory: The Civil War in Art* (1993), with Neely; *Lincoln on Democracy* (1990), with Mario M. Cuomo; *The Lincoln-Douglas Debates: The First Complete, Unexpurgated Text* (1993), *Washington and Lincoln Portrayed* (1993), *Dear Mr. Lincoln: Letters to the President* (1993), *Witness to War: The Civil War* (1996), *The Lincoln Mailbag* (1998), *The Union Preserved* (1999), and, for young readers, the two-volume set *The Civil War Era* (1996).

In addition, Holzer has written more than 270 articles for both popular magazines and scholarly journals, including *LIFE*, *American Heritage*, *Civil War Times Illustrated*, *America's Civil War*, *Blue & Gray*, *American History*, *MHQ*, *Illinois Historical Journal*, *The American Art Journal*, and *Winterthur Portfolio*. He regularly reviews Civil War books for the *Chicago Tribune*.

Holzer has written pamphlets and monographs on Lincoln; edited the "Books at Brown University" publication *Lincoln and Lincolniana* (1987); and contributed chapters to a number of books, including *Graphic Arts and the South* (1993), *The Encyclopedia of the Confederacy* (1993), and *We Cannot Escape History: Lincoln and the Last Best Hope of Earth* (1995). He delivered the Seventeenth Annual R. Gerald McMurtry Lecture at The Lincoln Museum, published in 1997 as "The Mirror Image of Civil War Memory: Abraham Lincoln and Jefferson Davis in Popular Prints."

Holzer served as consultant to the ABC-TV documentary miniseries *Lincoln*, broadcast in 1992, and appeared on camera on the 1992 PBS-TV documentary *Abraham Lincoln: A New Birth of Freedom*, in several episodes of the 1994 A&E series *Civil War Journals*, on the 1995 History Channel *Biography*, and in the History Channel special *Assassins: John Wilkes Booth*. Holzer's 1993 appearance on C-SPAN's *Booknotes* series inspired the re-creation of all seven Lincoln-Douglas debates in Illinois in 1994, for which Holzer served as historical consultant and on-air commentator. He has since appeared regularly on the C-SPAN network and lectures often at schools, museums, and Civil War and Lincoln groups.

LINCOLN PLACES TO VISIT

DISTRICT OF COLUMBIA
• Lincoln Memorial • Ford's Theatre National Historic Site
(includes The Petersen House)

ILLINOIS
Chicago
• Chicago Historical Society
Freeport
• Lincoln-Douglas Debate Square • Lincoln the Debater Statue
Petersburg
• Lincoln's New Salem State Historic Site
Springfield
• Lincoln Home National Historic Site • Old State Capitol
• Lincoln Herndon Law Offices State Historic Site • The Lincoln Depot
• Lincoln Tomb State Historic Site

INDIANA
Fort Wayne
• The Lincoln Museum
Lincoln City
• Lincoln Boyhood National Memorial

KENTUCKY
Hodgenville
• Abraham Lincoln Birthplace National Historic Site

NEW YORK
New York
• The Great Hall at The Cooper Union for the
Advancement of Science and Art
Westfield
• The Lincoln-Bedell Statue

PENNSYLVANIA
Gettysburg
• Gettysburg National Military Park